and Mixer
Recipes

GETTING IT RIGHT

Blender and Mixer Recipes

by Daphne Metland

foulsham

LONDON • NEW YORK • TORONTO • SYDNEY

foulsham
Yeovil Road, Slough, Berkshire, SL1 4JH

These recipes represent a small selection from:
Moulinex Blender & Mixer Cookbook

ISBN 0-572-01926-2

Printed in Great Britain by Cox & Wyman Ltd., Reading.

CONTENTS

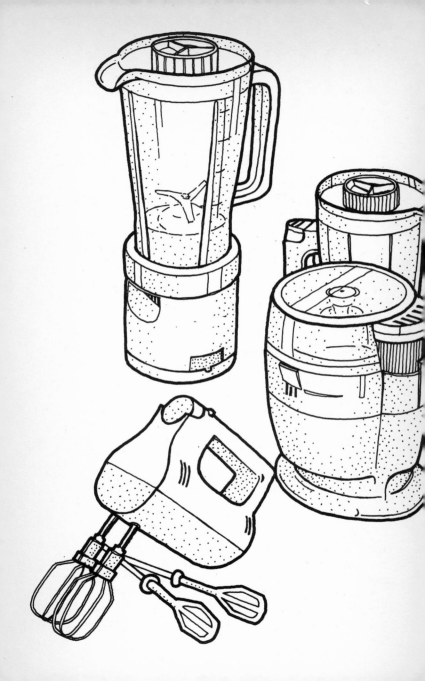

INTRODUCTION

Two or three generations ago, even the smallest of households had a cook, whose full time occupation was feeding the family. Now most of us have to juggle a variety of jobs, and cooking is just one of these, so any machine that saves time and effort in the kitchen is well worth having. Mixers and blenders of whatever size can do just that, allowing us to make more dishes in less time, with less effort.

Home baking is popular, and with a mixer to take the hard work out of making cakes and biscuits, it is a pleasure rather than a chore. Blenders can make almost instant sauces and soups, saving a great deal of time – as anyone who has laboriously sieved a soup will know. Many dishes that are normally complicated become simple and easy when a blender or mixer is to hand, allowing for more variety in cooking. Often leftover foods can be turned into complete meals, and gluts of fruits and vegetables can be used up as sauces, purées and mousses with a little help from kitchen machines, so they prove to be economical as well.

Keep any kitchen machine close to hand, and use them when experimenting with new dishes, as well as adapting tried and trusted recipes. The recipes in this book range from the familiar to the unusual, but all are quick and easy to tackle with the aid of your mixer or blender.

In most sections of the book we have included basic step by step recipes to show you how best to make, for example, soups, sauces or batter with your mixer and blender. Once you have mastered the basic techniques, try the variations on the basic skills provided by the recipes which follow. When you feel really confident experiment with recipes of your own.

VARIETIES OF BLENDERS AND MIXERS

The number and variety of kitchen machines has increased greatly over the past few years. Each family has different needs in the kitchen. Some of us have to cope with cooking for large numbers, some like to cook grand meals for entertaining, others like to batch bake for the freezer, and some of us need to cook for just one or two people most of the time. The variety of mixers and blenders on the market allows everyone to choose the ideal type of kitchen machine for their own needs. What each type can do varies slightly, but there are areas of overlap.

Food Mixers

These can be either hand held, or are available with a bowl and stand. Some small ones can be wall mounted, which is useful in a small kitchen. Some have one type of general purpose beater, others offer different beaters for whisking, creaming and making bread dough. Mixers that can be lifted off the stand and used in a saucepan, or in a bowl over a pan of hot water are the most versatile. They can also be used in a small bowl when mixing very small quantities of food, and some can be used with just one beater in place for this purpose.

Table-top mixers are much larger and heavier, and are best kept out on the worktop. They can cope with large-scale cooking and heavy duty work like making bread and fruit cakes. Many smaller mixers can also perform these tasks but on a smaller scale. Table-top mixers are ideal if you need to batch bake, or cope with large-scale cooking.

Hand Blenders

These are small hand-held machines with sharp blades in the end. They can be held in a saucepan, bowl or jug to purée foods such as sauces and soups, and are useful for small-scale cooking. They are ideal for making baby foods too.

Blenders

These are excellent general purpose kitchen machines that can cope with puréeing soft fruits and cooked vegetables, making soups, breadcrumbs, grinding nuts, making biscuit crumbs and pâtés. They are great time and effort savers in the kitchen, and can help produce meals in minutes that would take very much longer by hand.

Some smaller machines should only be used for the more liquid mixtures, but often these have a small-scale grinder or chopper as well. Some of the larger models also have a chopper fitment which will cope with chopping meats and hard vegetables.

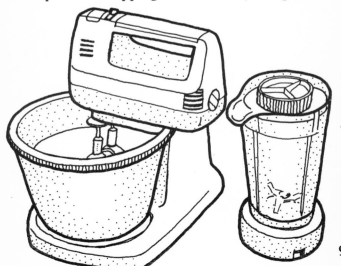

HOW TO USE
YOUR BLENDER

★ Make sure you only process those foods that are recommended in the instruction booklet that comes with your machine. This will vary depending on the type and size of machine.

★ Some foods need to be added through the centre of the lid with the machine running, so that the food drops onto the revolving blades and is cut up immediately. Generally this is the best technique to use for breadcrumbs, biscuit crumbs and grinding nuts. Mayonnaise and some other sauces are best made this way.

★ It may be necessary to stop the machine and scrape the food down from the sides of the blender goblet from time to time. This will ensure even blending with foods such as pâtés.

★ Some foods give best results when the blender is turned on and off several times rather than run constantly. Try this on/off technique for dry food and semi-solid foods.

★ Keep an eye on the consistency of the food. Blenders are very quick and powerful. With a little practice you will be able to control the fineness of the blending of foods such as nuts and breadcrumbs.

★ Some foods are better blended in batches, and some machines are smaller than others so foods will more often need blending in two or more smaller loads.

★ Look at the various jobs you need your blender to do for any one recipe. Arrange the order of work so that those foods that will make less mess are blended first, for example make breadcrumbs or chop herbs before making a sauce. All the recipes in this book have been arranged this way to minimise washing up.

★ Generally speaking it is better to place the liquid in any recipe in the blender first, and then add other ingredients. So for a batter, start with the milk in the blender and then add the flour and egg, so that all the food is mixed evenly.

HOW TO USE YOUR FOOD MIXER

★ Use the right beaters if there is a choice – the stronger beaters for creaming, the thinner ones for better aeration when whisking egg whites or cream.

★ Check in the instruction booklet what the machine is designed to cope with; some are simply hand-held whisks, ideal for whisking cream, egg whites and egg and sugar mixtures but not for any heavy duty cooking.

★ Have fats for creaming at room temperature so that they mix well and do not clog the beaters.

★ Choose a bowl of the right size for the mixture. Allow for the increase in volume of egg whites and cream.

★ When using a bowl on a stand, check that the mixture may need scraping down, as this is more likely than with a hand-held machine.

★ For mixtures that need whisking over a pan of hot water, check that the bowl is not actually touching the hot water or this may cause eggs to curdle.

SAFETY TIPS

Blenders

★ Always make sure the lid is firmly in place.

★ Never overload the machine, especially when blending hot liquids. The maximum amount to be blended will be less then the marking shown on the side of the blender as food rises up during blending, so check in the instruction booklet before use.

★ Check if the blender can withstand boiling liquids. Some can, others require foods to be removed from the heat and allowed to stand briefly before blending.

★ Always scrape out the blender using a plastic spatula. Never reach in with your finger to clear the blades of food.

Mixers

★ Always turn the mixer off before lifting the beaters out of the mixture to prevent splashing.

★ Make sure the beaters are firmly fitted into the machine before mixing.

★ Unplug the machine before removing the beaters to wash them.

Cleaning

The quickest way to clean a blender is to half fill it with warm water, add just a little washing up liquid, put the lid on and then blend briefly. For general use this is all that is needed. Only when blending foods such as pâtés and fruit purées will it be necessary to take the blender apart and clean it thoroughly. Wash in hot soapy water, and use a brush to clean the sharp blades. Dry thoroughly before re-assembling.

Mixers are easy to clean, since the beaters can be removed and washed in the washing up bowl. Again, use a brush to ensure the inside of the beaters are clean. Dry well.

The body of both blenders and mixers should never be immersed in water or made wet. Wipe wih a barely damp cloth, and if necessary use a little general purpose cream cleanser to remove food marks.

What not to put in your blender or mixer

Always check in your instruction booklet as each machine varies slightly.

As a general rule blenders cannot cope with coffee beans, whole ice cubes or whole wheat unless a special attachment is available. They should not be expected to cope with egg whites and other mixtures that need aeration, or solid mixtures such as cakes and bread dough.

Most mixers will be able to cope with cake mixes, pastry mixes and other jobs like mashing potatoes. However, beware of using lightweight whisks for cake or bread-making as they are not strong enough to cope.

WASTE NOT WANT NOT

Take advantage of your blender and food mixer to help you make the most of leftovers and use up gluts of food.

★ Use stale bread to make crumbs for stuffings, puddings and toppings. Either freeze, or dry in the oven on a baking tray and then use for coating foods.

★ Over-ripe fruits are often cheap, and can be used in purées and mousses, or even as a base for ice creams and sorbets.

★ Make a quick weekday lunch with home-made soup. The blender makes almost any soup very quick and easy. Cook seasonal or leftover vegetables in stock, then blend and reheat.

★ Stuffings stretch meat and make it go further. Make your own using the blender to produce breadcrumbs, and chop herbs, nuts and dried fruits.

★ Use up leftovers and stretch them by putting them in a sauce. Even a couple of ounces of leftover meat will feed the family if mixed with other ingredients such as bacon pieces, hard-boiled eggs etc. and coated in a well-flavoured sauce.

★ Home-made cakes and biscuits are cheaper than shop bought ones and generally much tastier. Make them easily and quickly using your food mixer.

★ Dress up a basic salad by adding a home-made dressing. Use the blender for quick mayonnaise and other dressings. Often the addition of a good dressing and a handful of nuts or cubed cheese can make a salad into a complete meal.

★ Use up leftovers by making a quick pizza. Use the mixer to make a scone mixture, then top with leftover ham, chicken and other meats. Add a few tinned tomatoes, herbs, seasonings and freshly grated cheese and cook in a hot oven until golden brown. Pizzas are good cold in packed lunches too.

TEN TIPS FOR USING YOUR BLENDER OR MIXER

★ Rescue lumpy sauces by blending briefly, then return to the pan and finish cooking.

★ Sauces that have been frozen and look rather unappetising on thawing often benefit from a quick whirl in the blender.

★ Egg-based sauces that begin to curdle can be rescued by standing the saucepan in a little cold water and then whisking well with the food mixer. Alternatively, tip into the blender and blend.

★ Freshly ground nuts have a better flavour than bought ground nuts, and whole nuts keep longer. So buy the whole variety and grind as needed.

★ It is possible to fold egg whites into a mixture that is already in the blender. Whisk the egg white separately, then add to the blender and blend for just a few seconds to incorporate it.

★ Milk shakes can be made quickly in the blender. Mix milk with whatever fruit is in season, and blend. For extra-creamy milk shakes add a scoop or two of ice cream and blend again.

★ Make quick, home-made cream in the blender using equal quantities of melted unsalted butter and milk. Blend and chill well before use.

★ Herbs will chop quickly and easily in the blender as long as they are dry. Wash and pat dry on kitchen paper. Remove any woody stems. Drop through the centre of the lid onto the revolving blade.

★ Instant batters can be made in one step in the blender. Simply place all ingredients into the blender, starting with the milk, and blend until smooth.

★ Pastry can be made using the mixer. This is very useful for anyone with warm hands as this often leads to heavy pastry. Try using the mixer to rub the fat into the flour until it resembles fine breadcrumbs. Then tip into a plastic box and store in the fridge until needed. It will keep for up to two weeks and can be removed by the tablespoon. Just add water as usual and roll out.

THE RECIPES

All the recipes in this book are designed to serve four, unless otherwise specified. The baby food recipes are for a single portion, although obviously this will vary with the age of the baby.

All spoon measurements are level, and based on a 5 ml teaspoon and a 15 ml tablespoon.

The symbols at the beginning of each recipe indicate whether they use a blender or a mixer. Recipes should be suitable for all blenders, but as specifications vary, you should read your own instruction booklet to check the capacity of your particular machine, whether to use the separate chopper etc.

 Suitable for freezing for the time specified. N.B. Dishes without this symbol are unsuitable for freezing.

 Recipe uses a blender.

 Recipe uses a mixer.

SOUPS

A blender is excellent for making quick soups. Use home-made stocks whenever possible for the best flavour. Blend the cooked ingredients in batches if necessary, depending on the size of your blender.

Celery Soup

INGREDIENTS	Metric	Imperial	American
Celery	450 g	1 lb	1 lb
Potato	1	1	1
Chicken stock	575 ml	1 pt	2½ cups
Caraway seeds	½ tsp	½ tsp	½ tsp
Salt and freshly ground black pepper			
Chopped parsley			

1. Wash the celery and chop. Place in a pan with the peeled chopped potato, the stock and caraway seeds. Season well.
2. Cook for 20 minutes until the vegetables are soft. Then blend until smooth. This may need to be done in batches.
3. Pour into serving dishes. Garnish with chopped parsley, or finely chopped tops of celery sticks.

Carrot and Lentil Soup

 4 months

INGREDIENTS	Metric	Imperial	American
Lentils	100 g	4 oz	¼ lb
Garlic	1 clove	1 clove	1 clove
Oil	15 ml	1 tbsp	1 tbsp
Onion	1	1	1
Carrots	450 g	1 lb	1 lb
Chicken stock	1.1 l	2 pt	5 cups
Salt and freshly ground black pepper			

Soak the lentils according to the instructions on the packet, or choose the no-soak variety. Crush the garlic and fry in the oil until brown, then add the chopped onion and fry gently. Scrub the carrots, slice and add to the onion. Add 850 ml/1½ pt/ 3¾ cups of stock, add the lentils and bring to the boil. Reduce the heat and simmer for 1 hour until the ingredients are soft. Add the remaining stock during this time if the soup becomes very thick.

Blend in batches until smooth and return to the pan. Reheat, adjust seasoning. Serve hot.

TO FREEZE
Cool and pour into a freezer container. Thaw for 5–6 hours at room temperature. Reheat in a saucepan without boiling.

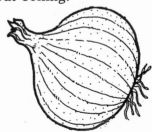

Tomato and Orange Soup

4 months

INGREDIENTS

	Metric	Imperial	American
Tomatoes	*450 g*	*1 lb*	*1 lb*
Potato	*1*	*1*	*1*
Carrot	*1*	*1*	*1*
Basil, fresh	*few sprigs*	*few sprigs*	*few sprigs*
OR *Dried*	*½ tsp*	*½ tsp*	*½ tsp*
Chicken stock	*850 ml*	*1½ pt*	*3¾ cups*
Salt and freshly ground black pepper			
Orange	*½*	*½*	*½*
Single (light) cream	*150 ml*	*¼ pt*	*⅔ cup*

Wipe the tomatoes and cut them in half. Peel the potato and carrot, and chop roughly. Place the vegetables, herbs and stock in a large pan. Season well. Bring to the boil and then simmer for 20 minutes. Blend, in two batches if necessary, and return to the pan. Heat, add the juice of the half orange. Check seasoning. Serve hot, pouring a little single cream into each dish.

TO FREEZE
Cool after blending, and add the orange juice. Freeze in a plastic container. Thaw for 4 hours at room temperature. Blend for a few seconds before reheating to give a smooth texture.

Leek and Stilton Soup

3 months

INGREDIENTS	Metric	Imperial	American
Leeks	*450 g*	*1 lb*	*1 lb*
Oil	*15 ml*	*1 tbsp*	*1 tbsp*
Potato	*1 large*	*1 large*	*1 large*
Chicken stock	*700 ml*	*1¼ pt*	*3 cups*
Salt and freshly ground black pepper			
Blue cheese	*50 g*	*2 oz*	*2 oz*

Trim and wash the leeks well, slice and fry in the oil until soft. Add the potato, roughly chopped, and the stock. Bring to the boil, reduce to simmer and cook for 15–20 minutes until the vegetables are soft. Blend the soup in two batches. With the last batch still in the blender, add the blue cheese, crumbled, to the blender and blend again. Mix this batch of soup with the other half, season well and serve immediately.

TO FREEZE
Do not add the cheese. Cool and pour into a freezer container. Thaw at room temperature for 5–6 hours, reheat, then pour into the blender and add the crumbled cheese as above.

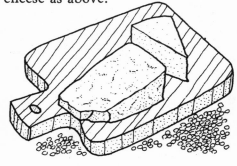

Kidney Soup

 3 months

INGREDIENTS	Metric	Imperial	American
Kidney	225 g	8 oz	½ lb
Onion	1	1	1
Butter	25 g	1 oz	2 tbsp
Tomato purée	5 ml	1 tsp	1 tsp
Carrot	1	1	1
Potato	1	1	1
Sherry	30–45 ml	2–3 tbsp	2–3 tbsp
Beef stock	850 ml	1½ pt	3¾ cups
Bay leaf	1	1	1
Salt and freshly ground black pepper			

Skin and core the kidneys. Soak in water for 1 hour, then drain and slice.

Fry the chopped onion in the butter until soft and brown. Add the tomato purée and stir well. Add the roughly chopped carrot and potato. Stir in the sherry, then the stock, kidney slices and bay leaf. Bring to the boil, reduce to simmer and cook for 50-60 minutes until tender. Season well.

Blend in batches, return to the pan and reheat. Serve hot.

TO FREEZE
Cool and pour into a freezer container. Thaw for 4–5 hours at room temperature. Reheat gently in a pan.

Iced Cucumber Soup

 2 months

INGREDIENTS	Metric	Imperial	American
Onion	1 small	1 small	1 small
Butter	15 g	½ oz	1 tbsp
Cucumber	1 large	1 large	1 large
Chicken stock	425 ml	¾ pt	2 cups
Egg yolk	1	1	1
Natural yoghurt	45 ml	3 tbsp	3 tbsp
Cornflour	2 tsp	2 tsp	2 tsp
Mint	few leaves	few leaves	few leaves

Lightly fry the onion in the butter until soft but not brown. Add the peeled cucumber, cut into slices, and the stock. Bring to the boil and simmer for 20 minutes.

Place the egg yolk, 15 ml/1 tbsp yoghurt and the cornflour in the blender and blend briefly to mix them. Then add the hot soup and blend again until smooth and creamy. Allow to cool.

Pour into small individual dishes and garnish with the remaining yoghurt and the chopped mint.

TO FREEZE
Pour into a freezer container. Thaw for 4–5 hours at room temperature. Blend before pouring into dishes and garnishing as above.

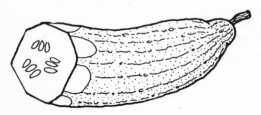

PÂTÉS AND STARTERS

Mushroom and Liver Pâté

INGREDIENTS	Metric	Imperial	American
Onion	1	1	1
Butter	50 g	2 oz	¼ cup
Mushrooms	50 g	2 oz	2 oz
Chicken livers	225 g	8 oz	½ lb
Calves' livers	450 g	1 lb	1 lb
Cream	60 ml	4 tbsp	4 tbsp
Ground mace	½ tsp	½ tsp	½ tsp
Salt and freshly ground black pepper			
Bay leaves	3	3	3

1. Chop the onion and fry in the butter until soft. Add the sliced mushrooms and fry lightly.
2. Chop the chicken livers and add to the pan, cook until just brown on the outside.
3. Prepare the calves' livers, removing any tubes. Cut up roughly and then blend until smooth.
4. Add the cooked chicken livers and vegetables. Blend.
5. Add the cream, mace and other seasonings and blend again.
6. Pour into a pâté dish, arrange the bay leaves on top and cover with a lid. Bake at 170°C/325°F/ Gas mark 3 for 1½ hours. Allow to cool, then leave overnight with weights on top of the pâté to press it down. Turn out of the dish, or serve in wedges from the dish.

Mackerel Pâté

 2 months

INGREDIENTS

	Metric	Imperial	American
Smoked mackerel	225 g	8 oz	½ lb
Lemon	½	½	½
Butter	50 g	2 oz	¼ cup
Soured cream	45 ml	3 tbsp	3 tbsp
Freshly ground black pepper			

Skin the mackerel and break into small pieces. Place in the blender with the juice of the half lemon, the melted butter and the soured cream. Season well with pepper and blend. Scrape down and blend again. Turn into a dish and chill for 1-2 hours. Serve cold.

TO FREEZE
Cover and freeze. Thaw overnight for 6–8 hours.

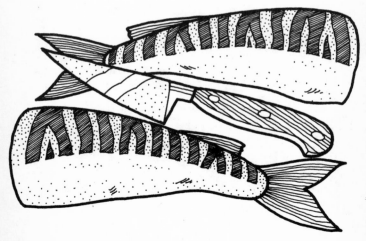

Country Pork Pâté

 4 months

INGREDIENTS	Metric	Imperial	American
Garlic	1 clove	1 clove	1 clove
Oil	15 ml	1 tbsp	1 tbsp
Onion	1 med	1 med	1 med
Butter	50 g	2 oz	¼ cup
Streaky bacon	175 g	6 oz	6 oz
Chicken livers	100 g	4 oz	¼ lb
Pigs' liver	225 g	8 oz	½ lb
Freshly ground black pepper			
Mace	¼ tsp	¼ tsp	¼ tsp
Cream	30 ml	2 tbsp	2 tbsp
Sherry	10 ml	2 tsp	2 tsp
Minced pork	225 g	8 oz	½ lb

Crush the garlic and fry in the oil. Add the chopped onion and fry until soft. Add the butter to melt it, then remove from the heat.

Use half the bacon to line an ovenproof dish. Chop the remaining bacon finely. Wipe and slice the livers, removing any tubes. Place both types of liver in the blender and blend until smooth. Add the butter and onion mixture and blend again. Add the pepper, mace, cream and sherry and blend again.

Put the chopped bacon and minced pork in a large bowl and pour on the contents of the blender. Mix well. Pour into the lined ovenproof dish. Cover with foil or a lid and bake at 180°C/350°F/Gas mark 4 for 1½–2 hours. Place a weight on top of the pâté to press it and allow to stand overnight.

TO FREEZE

Cool, then overwrap. Thaw for 6 hours at room temperature. Or it can be frozen in slices for quicker thawing: allow 1–2 hours.

Chicken and Orange Pâté

 2–3 months

INGREDIENTS

	Metric	Imperial	American
Garlic	1 clove	1 clove	1 clove
Butter	100 g	4 oz	½ cup
Onion	1 large	1 large	1 large
Chicken livers	450 g	1 lb	1 lb
Sherry	30 ml	2 tbsp	2 tbsp
Orange	1	1	1
Cream	125 ml	4 fl oz	½ cup

Crush the garlic clove and fry in the butter. Finely chop the onion, add to the garlic and fry gently until brown. Chop the chicken livers, add to the onion and fry for 3–4 minutes until brown. Add the sherry and stir well. Place the contents of the pan in the blender, add the juice of the orange and blend. You may need to do this in two batches. Pour in the cream and blend again. Spoon into individual dishes, smooth the tops and chill for 1 hour. Serve chilled with toast as a starter.

TO FREEZE

Overwrap before freezing. Thaw overnight in the fridge or for 3–4 hours at room temperature.

Smoked Haddock Mousse

 2 months

INGREDIENTS	Metric	Imperial	American
Smoked haddock	*350 g*	*12 oz*	*¾ lb*
Milk	*275 ml*	*½ pt*	*1¼ cups*
Flour	*25 g*	*1 oz*	*¼ cup*
Margarine	*25 g*	*1 oz*	*2 tbsp*
Salt and freshly ground black pepper			
Eggs	*2*	*2*	*2*
Mayonnaise	*30 ml*	*2 tbsp*	*2 tbsp*
Gelatine	*15 g*	*¼ oz*	*1 sachet*
Water	*30 ml*	*2 tbsp*	*2 tbsp*

Poach the haddock in 150 ml/¼ pt/⅔ cup of milk. Remove from the skin and break up when cooked.

Make a sauce using the cooking liquid from the fish made up with milk to 425 ml/¾ pt/2 cups, plus the flour and margarine. Blend all the ingredients together, then pour into a pan and cook until it thickens. Season well. Return to the blender. Blend.

Separate the eggs and add the yolks to the sauce. Blend again. Add the fish and blend. Turn into a bowl to cool. Then add the mayonnaise. Dissolve the packet of gelatine in the water. Whisk the egg whites. Mix the gelatine into the fish mixture and then fold in the egg whites.

Turn into a 1 1/2 pt mould. Leave to set.

TO FREEZE
Make in a freezerproof mould, overwrap and freeze in the mould. Thaw overnight in the fridge.

Shrimp Toasts

 1 month

INGREDIENTS	Metric	Imperial	American
Bread	5 slices	5 slices	5 slices
Shrimps	100 g	4 oz	¼ lb
Butter	50 g	2 oz	¼ cup
Curry paste	½ tsp	½ tsp	½ tsp
Coriander	pinch	pinch	pinch
Parsley	few sprigs	few sprigs	few sprigs

Make one slice of bread into breadcrumbs in the blender. Roll a rolling pin over the remaining slices of bread to flatten them slightly and then cut rounds from them using a biscuit cutter. Toast the rounds lightly.

Reserve a few shrimps for garnish. Chop the remaining shrimps in the blender, add the butter, cut into pieces, and blend to incorporate. Turn into a bowl, add the breadcrumbs and mix well. Stir in the curry paste and coriander. Divide the mixture between the toast rounds and grill under a hot grill for 5–6 minutes until golden. Garnish with the reserved shrimps and the parsley.

Serve hot as a starter or with drinks.

TO FREEZE
Freeze before toasting. Open freeze until hard then transfer to a freezer box. Thaw for 2 hours at room temperature, then grill as above.

Prawn and Rice Ring

INGREDIENTS	Metric	Imperial	American
Long grain rice	400 g	14 oz	14 oz
Lemon juice	10 ml	2 tsp	2 tsp
Oil	5 ml	1 tsp	1 tsp
Butter	15 g	½ oz	1 tbsp
Celery	4 sticks	4 sticks	4 sticks
Oil	15 ml	1 tbsp	1 tbsp
Red pepper	1	1	1
Bean sprouts	75 g	3 oz	3 oz
Prawns	175 g	6 oz	6 oz
Sherry	15 ml	1 tbsp	1 tbsp
Tinned tomatoes	small tin	small tin	small tin

Cook the long grain rice with the lemon juice in plenty of boiling salted water for 12 minutes. Drain well, and rinse with plenty of hot water.

Lightly oil a 1 1/2 pt metal ring mould and press the rice into this. Cut the butter into pieces and distribute on top. Cover with foil and bake at 200°C/400°F/Gas mark 6 for 10–15 minutes.

Finally chop the celery and fry in the oil in a wide-based pan. Slice the pepper finely, add half to the celery and stir fry for 2–3 minutes. Add the bean sprouts and prawns and stir fry for 2–3 minutes. Add the sherry.

Blend the tinned tomatoes and the remaining half of the red pepper until smooth. Pour into the pan and cook for 4–5 minutes.

Turn the rice ring out onto a flat plate. Loosen the edges of the rice with a palette knife, cover the ring with a plate and turn upside down. Shake sharply so that the ring falls onto the plate. Remove the ring mould.

Pour the prawn and vegetable mixture into the middle of the ring and serve immediately.

Serve as a starter or lunch dish.

NOTE
Do not freeze.

Stuffed Tomatoes

INGREDIENTS	Metric	Imperial	American
Tomatoes	4 large	4 large	4 large
Prawns or shrimps	100 g	4 oz	¼ lb
Curd cheese or cream cheese	100 g	4 oz	¼ lb
Cream	15 ml	1 tbsp	1 tbsp
Tabasco sauce	½ tsp	½ tsp	½ tsp
Salt and freshly ground pepper			
Spring onions	4	4	4
To garnish			
Chopped chives	1 tbsp	1 tbsp	1 tbsp
Watercress	bunch	bunch	bunch

Cut the tomatoes in half and scoop out the seeds. Reserve 8 prawns or shrimps for garnish. Place the rest in the blender and chop finely, scraping down as necessary. Add the cheese, cut into pieces, the cream and the tabasco. Season well, and blend until smooth. Add the finely chopped spring onions. Pipe or spoon into the tomato shells. Top with reserved prawns or shrimps and chopped chives. Serve on a flat plate with plenty of dark green watercress.

NOTE
Do not freeze.

MAIN MEALS

From family favourites like lasagne and warming beef
casserole to more elaborate dinner party dishes like
Turkey Wellington and Guard of Honour, your mixer
and blender can help you prepare successful meals
more quickly and easily.

Rich Beef Casserole with Parsley Dumplings

5 months

INGREDIENTS	Metric	Imperial	American
Braising steak	450 g	1 lb	1 lb
Oil	15–30 ml	1–2 tbsp	1–2 tbsp
Onion	1	1	1
Mushrooms	50 g	2 oz	2 oz
Carrot	1	1	1
Juniper berries	2	2	2
Beef stock	575 ml	1 pt	2½ cups
Worcestershire sauce	3–4 drops	3–4 drops	3–4 drops
Parsley	few sprigs	few sprigs	few sprigs
Self-raising flour	100 g	4 oz	1 cup
Shredded suet	50 g	2 oz	2 oz
Salt and freshly ground black pepper			
Water	60–75 ml	4–5 tbsp	4–5 tbsp

Trim the meat and cut into cubes. Brown in the oil in two batches. Remove from the pan. Chop the onion and fry until brown. Add the sliced mushrooms and cook for 2–3 minutes. Add the peeled and sliced carrot and the meat. Crush the juniper berries between two teaspoons and add to the stock with the Worcestershire sauce. Pour round the meat. Cook until tender either on the top of the stove, or in the oven at 180°C/350°F/Gas mark 4 for 1½ hours.

Chop the parsley in the blender. Place the flour, suet, parsley and salt and pepper in a large bowl. Use the mixer to mix in 60–75 ml/4–5 tbsp of water until the dough holds together. Form into 8 small balls.

Remove the meat from the casserole using a slotted spoon. Pour the stock and vegetables into the blender and blend until smooth and thick. You may need to do this in two batches. If the sauce is very thick, add a little water to thin it to the right consistency. Return the meat to the casserole dish, pour round the sauce and place the dumplings around the edge. Bake at 200°C/400°F/Gas mark 6 for 20–30 minutes until the dumplings are brown.

This dish can be made the day before and left ready to add the freshly-made dumplings and reheat.

TO FREEZE
Freeze without the dumplings, in a freezer container. Thaw for 6–8 hours at room temperature, then add the dumplings and reheat at 200°C/400°F/ Gas mark 6 for 30 minutes.

Kidney and Mushroom Lasagne

 3 months

INGREDIENTS	Metric	Imperial	American
Calves' or pigs' kidneys	450 g	1 lb	1 lb
Onion	1	1	1
Oil	15 ml	1 tbsp	1 tbsp
Mushrooms	100 g	4 oz	¼ lb
Sherry	30 ml	2 tbsp	2 tbsp
Tomato purée	15 ml	1 tbsp	1 tbsp
Plain flour	15 g	½ oz	2 tbsp
Stock	425 ml	¾ pt	2 cups
Salt and freshly ground black pepper			
Milk	575 ml	1 pt	2½ cups
Flour	40 g	1½ oz	3 tbsp
Margarine	40 g	1½ oz	1½ tbsp
Nutmeg	½ tsp	½ tsp	½ tsp
Lasagne	6 slices	6 slices	6 slices
Parmesan cheese	1 tbsp	1 tbsp	1 tbsp

Remove any excess fat from the kidneys, skin, cut through and remove the core. Wash, pat dry and cut into pieces. Set aside.

Slice the onion and fry in half the oil. Add half the sliced mushrooms and fry gently. Add the sherry, tomato purée, flour and stock. Season well. Bring to the boil and cook for 10 minutes with the lid off the pan. Remove from the heat, cool slightly and then pour into the blender. Blend until smooth.

Fry the kidney slices in the remaining oil, add the reserved mushrooms, and then pour the sauce round them. Simmer for 5 minutes.

35

Make the bechamel sauce by placing the milk, flour and margarine in the blender. Blend until well combined then pour into a pan and bring to the boil, stirring continuously. Once thickened, add the nutmeg and season well.

Cook the lasagne according to the instructions on the packet.

Pour the kidneys in their sauce into a shallow ovenproof dish. Arrange the lasagne slices on top, then pour the bechamel sauce over. Sprinkle the parmesan on top. Bake at 200°C/400°F/Gas mark 6 for 20–30 minutes.

TO FREEZE

Prepare in a freezerproof dish. Cool, then overwrap. Thaw for 6–8 hours at room temperature and bake as above or cook from frozen at 180°C/350°F/Gas mark 4 for 50–60 minutes.

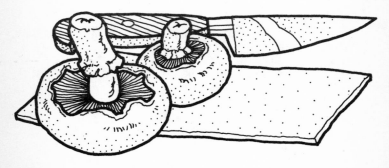

Lamb in Rich Spicy Sauce

 1 month

INGREDIENTS	Metric	Imperial	American
Garlic	1 clove	1 clove	1 clove
Oil	15 ml	1 tbsp	1 tbsp
Onion	1 large	1 large	1 large
Rogan josh curry powder	3 tsp	3 tsp	3 tsp
Tinned tomatoes	400 g	14 oz	1 med tin
Tomato purée	15 ml	1 tbsp	1 tbsp
Lemon juice	15 ml	1 tbsp	1 tbsp
Mango chutney	1 tbsp	1 tbsp	1 tbsp
Garam masala spices	2 tsp	2 tsp	2 tsp
Natural yoghurt	50 ml	2 fl oz	¼ cup
Cooked lamb	450 g	1 lb	1 lb

Fry the crushed garlic in the oil. Chop the onion
and fry half with the garlic until brown. Add the
rogan josh curry powder and cook for 1–2 minutes,
then add the tin of tomatoes, the tomato purée,
lemon juice and mango chutney. Cook gently for
15–20 minutes. Pour into the blender, add the
garam masala spices and blend. Add the natural
yoghurt and blend again. Return the sauce to the
pan, add the chopped lamb and the remaining
onion. Bring to the boil, reduce the heat and
simmer for 10–15 minutes.

Serve with rice and extra mango chutney.

TO FREEZE
Cool, then pack into a plastic box. Thaw for 4–5
hours at room temperature. Reheat in a pan for 15
minutes.

Chicken Escalopes with Cream and Wine Sauce

INGREDIENTS	Metric	Imperial	American
Parsley	few sprigs	few sprigs	few sprigs
Bread	100 g	4 oz	4 slices
Chicken breasts	4	4	4
Egg	1	1	1
Milk	15 ml	1 tbsp	1 tbsp
Salt and freshly ground black pepper			
Oil	45 ml	3 tbsp	3 tbsp
Butter	50 g	2 oz	¼ cup
Wine	60 ml	4 tbsp	4 tbsp
Lemon juice	10 ml	2 tsp	2 tsp
Cream	60 ml	4 tbsp	4 tbsp

Chop the parsley in the blender. Make the bread into crumbs in batches. Mix the parsley and crumbs on a large plate.

Beat the chicken breasts with a wooden rolling pin to flatten them slightly. Break the egg into a shallow dish, beat lightly with the milk and season well. Dip the chicken in the egg and then press down into the breadcrumbs. Fry in the oil for 4–5 minutes each side. Lift out onto a warm serving dish.

Melt the butter in the pan, add the wine and lemon juice and stir well to collect all the pan juices. Add the cream and stir round, then pour over the chicken breasts and serve immediately.

NOTE
Do not freeze.

Sweet and Sour Chicken

INGREDIENTS

	Metric	Imperial	American
Carrots	2	2	2
Tinned pineapple	150 g	5 oz	½ tin
Brown sugar	2 tsp	2 tsp	2 tsp
Wine vinegar	15 ml	1 tbsp	1 tbsp
Soy sauce	15 ml	1 tbsp	1 tbsp
Water	275 ml	½ pt	1¼ cups
Cornflour	1 tbsp	1 tbsp	1 tbsp
Yeast, fresh	15 g	¼ oz	¼ oz
Warm water	150 ml	¼ pt	⅔ cup
Oil	5 ml	1 tsp	1 tsp
Plain flour	100 g	4 oz	1 cup
Egg	1	1	1
Boned chicken breasts	2	2	2

Wash and grate the carrots. Purée the pineapples and their juice in the blender. Add the sugar, wine vinegar, soy sauce and 275 ml/½ pt/1¼ cups of water and blend. Pour into a pan and cook for 10 minutes. Mix the cornflour with a little water to form a smooth paste. Pour the hot sauce on the cornflour mixture, and stir well. Return to the pan and bring to the boil, stirring well. Remove from the heat.

Place the yeast in the blender with the warm water and blend. Add the oil, plain flour and egg yolk and blend. Allow to stand for 20 minutes. Whisk the egg white, using the mixer, and add to the blender. Blend for just long enough to incorporate the egg white.

Cut the chicken breasts into strips or cubes. Dip each piece into the batter and fry in hot oil

until light, fluffy and brown, about 4-5 mintues.
Drain well. This may need to be done in batches.

Serve with the sweet and sour sauce, and rice,
noodles or beansprouts.

NOTE
Do not freeze.

Turkey Wellington

INGREDIENTS	Metric	Imperial	American
Bread	25 g	1 oz	1 slice
Raw turkey roll	450–550 g	1–1¼ lb	1–1¼ lb
Turkey livers	100 g	4 oz	¼ lb
Mushrooms	50 g	2 oz	2 oz
Butter	25 g	1 oz	1 tbsp
Salt and freshly ground black pepper			
Frozen puff pastry	450 g	1 lb	1 lb
Egg	1	1	1

Make the bread into crumbs in the blender.

Remove the fat or inner wrapping from the
turkey roll. Place the livers in the blender and blend
until roughly chopped. Wipe the mushrooms and
chop. Add to the livers and blend. Cut the butter
into pieces, add and blend again. Season well and
add the breadcrumbs. Blend to mix all the
ingredients.

Roll out the pastry to make a rectangle about
25 cm × 40 cm/10 × 16 ins. Place half the liver
mixture in the middle of the pastry. Sit the turkey
roll on top. Spread the rest of the liver mixture over
the turkey roll. Fold the pastry over to make a

parcel, fold the ends in and press down well. Glaze with beaten egg. Turn the parcel over onto a baking tray so that the joins in the pastry are underneath. Glaze the top with beaten egg, cut steam vents and decorate with pastry leaves.

Bake at 220°C/425°F/Gas mark 7 for 20 minutes until the pastry is brown and crisp. Reduce the heat to 190°C/375°F/Gas mark 5 for a further 45–50 minutes. Serve hot or cold.

NOTE
Do not freeze.

Guard of Honour

INGREDIENTS	Metric	Imperial	American
Best end of neck (cut in two pieces, each having 6 to 8 chops)	*900 g*	*2 lb*	*2 lb*
Bread	*50 g*	*2 oz*	*2 slices*
Pork sausagemeat	*225 g*	*8 oz*	*½ lb*
Mushrooms	*50 g*	*2 oz*	*2 oz*
Lemon juice	*5 ml*	*1 tsp*	*1 tsp*
Mustard	*½ tsp*	*½ tsp*	*½ tsp*
Salt and freshly ground black pepper			
Tomatoes	*4 med*	*4 med*	*4 med*
Rosemary	*2–3 sprigs*	*2–3 sprigs*	*2–3 sprigs*
Butter	*50 g*	*2 oz*	*¼ cup*
Lemon juice	*5 ml*	*1 tsp*	*1 tsp*
Mustard	*1 tsp*	*1 tsp*	*1 tsp*
Garlic	*1 clove*	*1 clove*	*1 clove*

Ask the butcher remove the chine bone from the meat. Then cut off the top 2.5 cm/ 1 inch of fat at the thin end, leaving the bones exposed. Discard the fat. Trim the meat between the bones, and scrape each bone to clean it. Chop this meat finely and keep it to one side.

Make the bread into crumbs in the blender. Place the pork sausagemeat in a large bowl, mash well with a fork and add the breadcrumbs. Wash and roughly chop the mushrooms, then finely chop in the blender. Add these to the sausagemeat, with the lemon juice, mustard and meat. Season well. Cut each tomato in half and scoop out the seeds. Place the seeds in the blender and blend until just broken up, then add to the sausagement. Mix well. Use half of this mixture to fill the tomato shells.

Stand the lamb pieces so that the exposed bones interlock. Form the stuffing into a thick sausage and place in the middle of the two pieces of lamb. Place in a shallow ovenproof dish.

Strip the rosemary leaves from the woody stem and chop them in the blender. Mix with the butter, lemon juice, mustard and crushed garlic. Score lines on the fatty side of the meat with a sharp knife and spread the butter mixture over the outside. Cook at 190°C/375°F/Gas mark 5 for 50–60 minutes. Add the tomatoes to the dish after the first 30 minutes.

NOTE
Do not freeze.

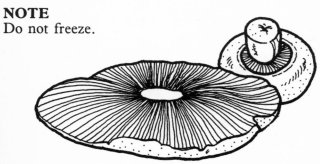

SUPPER DISHES

The recipes in this section make ideal light lunch and supper dishes. Follow the step by step guide to making batter, and use it to make Whomemeal Pancake Stack which is sure to become a favourite.

Batter Mixture

Smooth lump-free batters are quick and easy in the blender. For fritter batters, whisk the egg white separately and add at the end, mixing it into the batter by turning the blender on and off for short bursts.

INGREDIENTS	Metric	Imperial	American
Milk	275 ml	½ pt	1¼ cups
Egg	1	1	1
Plain flour	100 g	4 oz	1 cup

1. Place the milk in the blender first, then add the egg and finally the flour. This prevents the dry ingredients collecting at the base of the blender.
2. Blend for 10–15 seconds until smooth.
3. Pour out and use for Yorkshire puddings, toad in the hole or pancakes.

Wholemeal Pancake Stack

INGREDIENTS	Metric	Imperial	American
Cashew nuts (unsalted)	50 g	2 oz	2 oz
Milk	275 ml	½ pt	1¼ cups
Plain flour	50 g	2 oz	½ cup
Wholemeal flour	50 g	2 oz	½ cup
Egg	1	1	1
Oil for frying			
Garlic	1 clove	1 clove	1 clove
Leek	1	1	1
OR Spring onions	6	6	6
Red pepper	½	½	½
Green pepper	½	½	½
Courgette	1	1	1
Tomato	1	1	1
Bean sprouts	225 g	8 oz	½ lb
Streaky bacon	4 slices	4 slices	4 slices
Salad oil	30 ml	2 tbsp	2 tbsp
Prawns	50 g	2 oz	2 oz
Soy sauce	30 ml	2 tbsp	2 tbsp
Sherry	45 ml	3 tbsp	2 tbsp

Grind the nuts in the blender, then add the milk, flour and egg. Blend until smooth. Use to make 6 pancakes, set aside.

Prepare all the vegetables before beginning to cook them. Crush the garlic clove, trim the leek, wash well and slice, or chop the spring onion. Deseed the peppers, slice thinly, blanch in boiling water for 2 minutes then drain and rinse with cold water. Slice the courgette and cut the tomato into 8. Soak the bean sprouts for 10 minutes in cold water, then drain. Derind the bacon and cut into small strips.

Heat the salad oil in a wok or large frying pan. Fry the garlic until lightly browned, add the leek or spring onions, stir well. Then add the bacon and cook until brown. Stir in the courgette slices, peppers and the prawns and cook for about 1 minute, then add the tomatoes and bean sprouts and stir all the ingredients together. Mix the soy sauce and sherry together and add to the pan. Stir well.

Place one pancake in a flat ovenproof dish, spread a quarter of the cooked mixture on top and then place another pancake on top. Continue stacking pancakes and filling, finishing with a pancake. Cover with foil and bake at 190°C/375°F/Gas mark 5 for 10 minutes. Cut into wedges and serve immediately.

NOTE
Do not freeze.

Bacon Stuffed Cabbage Leaves

 2 months

INGREDIENTS

	Metric	Imperial	American
Onion	1 small	1 small	1 small
Oil	15 ml	1 tbsp	1 tbsp
Mushrooms	25 g	1 oz	1 oz
Bacon	225 g	8 oz	½ lb
Bread	50 g	1 oz	1 slice
Cashew nuts	50 g	2 oz	2 oz
Long grain rice	50 g	2 oz	2 oz
Large cabbage leaves	8–10	8–10	8–10
Pimentos	small tin	small tin	small tin

Salt and freshly ground
   black pepper
Tinned tomatoes   400 g   14 oz   med tin

Chop the onion finely and fry in the oil until
brown. Wash and slice the mushrooms, add to the
onion and fry. Derind the bacon, cut up and fry
lightly. Remove from the heat. In the blender, make
the bread into crumbs and chop the cashews. Cook
the rice in boiling salted water for 12 minutes, drain
well and rinse. Pour boiling water over the cabbage
leaves and leave to stand for 5 minutes to soften
them.

Drain the tin of pimentos and cut half into
pieces. Mix the rice, breadcrumbs, cashews and
pimentos into the cooked bacon mixture. Season
well and use to stuff the leaves. Place each rolled
leaf with the join side down in a shallow dish.

Place the remaining pimentos in the blender,
add the tin of tomatoes and blend until smooth.
Pour this over the cabbage leaves.

Cover the dish with foil and bake at
180°C/350°F/Gas mark 4 for 45 minutes. Serve
hot.

TO FREEZE
Cool the cooked dish. Place in a freezer box. Thaw
for 6–8 hours at room temperature. Reheat at
200°C/400°F/Gas mark 6 for 20–25 minutes.

Chicken and Sweetcorn Samosas

INGREDIENTS	Metric	Imperial	American
Cooked chicken	100 g	4 oz	1/4 lb
Sweetcorn	50 g	2 oz	2 oz
Milk	150 ml	1/4 pt	2/3 cup
Flour	1 tbsp	1 tbsp	1 tbsp
Butter	15 g	1/2 oz	1 tbsp
Salt and freshly ground black pepper			
Egg	1	1	1
Frozen puff pastry	450 g	1 lb	1 lb
Fat for frying			

Finely chop the chicken and mix with the sweetcorn. Place the milk, flour and butter in the blender and blend until well combined. Season, pour into a pan and bring to the boil, stirring well. Remove from the heat and beat in half the egg. Add the chicken and sweetcorn.

Roll out the puff pastry as thinly as possible into a large rectangle. Divide into 8 small rectangles. Place a teaspoon of the chicken mixture into each rectangle, glaze the edges and fold over to make a square parcel. Seal the edges well by folding them over and then glaze both sides.

Chill for 30 minutes. Then cook in deep fat, frying for 5–6 minutes until golden brown and well puffed. Drain well. Serve immediately.

NOTE
Do not freeze.

Stuffed Eggs

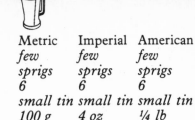

INGREDIENTS	Metric	Imperial	American
Parsley	few sprigs	few sprigs	few sprigs
Large eggs	6	6	6
Tinned tuna	small tin	small tin	small tin
Cream cheese	100 g	4 oz	¼ lb
Butter	50 g	2 oz	¼ cup
Freshly ground black pepper			
Tomatoes	2	2	2
Lemon	1	1	1

Chop the parsley in the blender, then remove. Hard boil the eggs, shell and cut in half lengthwise. Scoop out the yolks. Place the whites in a bowl of water to prevent them going hard. Drain the can of tuna and place in the blender. Add the cream cheese, cut into pieces, and the egg yolks. Melt the butter and pour into the blender. Blend until smooth, scraping down if necessary. Add the chopped parsley and season well with plenty of freshly ground black pepper. Blend again. Pipe the mixture into the whites of the egg, or fill the whites with a teaspoon. Arrange on a flat plate.

Fill the centre of the circle of eggs with tomatoes cut into slices or wedges. Finally add the lemon cut into thin wedges. Alternatively, you can garnish with fresh watercress.

Serve as a starter or lunch dish.

NOTE
Do not freeze.

Cannelloni Stuffed with Spinach

⚘ 4 months

INGREDIENTS

	Metric	Imperial	American
Spinach, fresh	450 g	1 lb	1 lb
OR Frozen	225 g	8 oz	½ lb
Cream cheese	100 g	4 oz	¼ lb
Salt and freshly ground black pepper			
Cannelloni tubes	12	12	12
Wholemeal bread	25 g	1 oz	1 slice
Milk	575 ml	1 pt	2½ cups
Flour	40 g	1½ oz	1½ tbsp
Butter	40 g	1½ oz	3 tbsp
Nutmeg	½ tsp	½ tsp	½ tsp

If using fresh spinach, wash very well, then cook for 6–7 minutes in just a little boiling salted water. Drain well. Purée in the blender. If using frozen spinach, thaw, heat through, and purée in the blender. Add the cream cheese, cut into pieces, to the spinach in the blender and blend to combine. Season well. Use this mixture to fill the cannelloni tubes. Place in a shallow ovenproof dish in one layer. Make the bread into crumbs in the blender. Remove.

Place the milk, flour, butter and nutmeg in the blender and blend until well combined. Pour into a pan and heat, stirring, until the sauce boils. Then pour over the cannelloni. Sprinkle the breadcrumbs on top and cook at 200°C/400°F/Gas mark 6 for 30–40 minutes until golden brown on top.

TO FREEZE

Cook, then allow to cool. Thaw for 5–6 hours at room temperature. Reheat at 200°C/400°F/Gas mark 6 for 20 minutes.

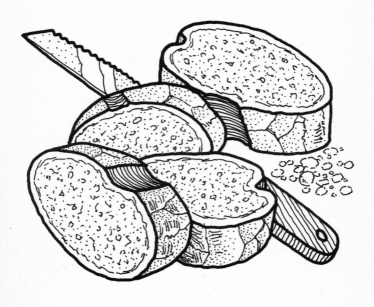

FISH

Seafood Soufflé

INGREDIENTS	Metric	Imperial	American
Bread	½ slice	½ slice	½ slice
Haddock	225 g	8 oz	½ lb
Milk	150 ml	¼ pt	⅔ cup
Butter	15 g	½ oz	1 tbsp
Flour	15 g	½ oz	2 tbsp
Salt and freshly ground black pepper			
Eggs	3	3	3
Prawns	100 g	4 oz	¼ lb
Grated cheese	25 g	1 oz	1 oz

Make the bread into crumbs in the blender. Set aside. Poach the haddock in the milk for about 8 minutes. Remove the fish. Pour the milk into the blender, add the butter and flour and blend. Season well. Pour into a pan and cook until thick. Draw aside from the heat and add the egg yolks. Beat well. Remove the skin from the haddock and break up the flesh. Add to sauce along with the prawns. Whisk the egg whites and fold into the sauce. Turn into a well buttered 18 cm/7 inch soufflé dish. Sprinkle with the breadcrumbs and cheese. Bake at 200°C/400°F/Gas mark 6 for 30–35 minutes until well risen and brown. Serve hot as a lunch or supper dish.

Vary the fish according to taste.

NOTE
Do not freeze.

Fish Cakes

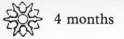 4 months

INGREDIENTS	Metric	Imperial	American
Bread	50 g	2 oz	2 slices
Parsley	few sprigs	few sprigs	few sprigs
Potatoes	450 g	1 lb	1 lb
White fish (cod, coley, haddock etc.)	350 g	12 oz	¾ lb
Milk	150 ml	¼ pt	⅔ cup
Nutmeg	¼ tsp	¼ tsp	¼ tsp
Salt and freshly ground black pepper			
Egg	1	1	1
Oil for frying			

Make the bread into crumbs in the blender. Remove. Chop the parsley in the blender. Cook the potatoes in boiling salted water until tender. Drain well and mash, using the mixer. Poach the fish in the milk for 8–10 minutes. Lift the fish out, skin, and then place the milk, cooking liquor and fish in the blender and blend for just a few seconds to break up the fish. Mix the fish mixture with the mashed potatoes. Add the parsley and nutmeg, season well and shape the mixture into balls. Flatten each one slightly, then dip in the beaten egg and roll in the breadcrumbs. Chill for 30 minutes. Fry in shallow fat for 3–4 minutes each side.
Makes 8–10.

TO FREEZE
Open freeze until hard then pack into a freezer bag or box. Thaw for 1–2 hours at room temperature.

Family Fish Pie

✲ 2 months

INGREDIENTS

	Metric	Imperial	American
Potatoes	*700 g*	*1½ lb*	*1½ lb*
Parsley	*few sprigs*	*few sprigs*	*few sprigs*
White fish (cod, coley or haddock)	*350 g*	*12 oz*	*¾ lb*
Milk	*275 ml*	*½ pt*	*1¼ cups*
Butter	*50 g*	*2 oz*	*¼ cup*
Flour	*25 g*	*1 oz*	*¼ cup*
Salt and freshly ground black pepper			
Milk	*30 ml*	*2 tbsp*	*2 tbsp*
Nutmeg	*½ tsp*	*½ tsp*	*½ tsp*
Prawns or shrimps	*50 g*	*2 oz*	*2 oz*
Grated cheese	*25 g*	*1 oz*	*1 oz*

Peel the potatoes, cut up and boil until tender. Chop the parsley in the blender.

Poach the fish in 150 ml/¼ pt/⅔ cup of milk for 8–10 minutes. Remove the fish, skin and break up. Put the cooking liquid, plus the remaining 150 ml/¼ pt/⅓ cup of milk, half the butter and the flour in the blender. Blend until smooth. Pour into a pan and bring to the boil, stirring. Season and stir in the parsley and fish. Stir well.

Drain the potatoes and mash with the 30 ml/2 tbsp of milk and the remaining butter. Add nutmeg to taste. Spread half the potatoes on the base of an ovenproof dish. Distribute the prawns or shrimps on top, then pour on the fish and sauce. Sprinkle the grated cheese on top. Pipe the remaining potato

around the edge of the dish and bake at 200°C/
400°F/Gas mark 6 for 20–30 minutes until hot and
lightly browned.

TO FREEZE
Cool, then overwrap. Thaw for 4–5 hours at room
temperature. Reheat at 200°C/400°F/Gas mark 6
for 20 minutes.

Gougons of Plaice with Tartare Sauce

INGREDIENTS	Metric	Imperial	American
Plain flour	100 g	4 oz	1 cup
Egg	1	1	1
Oil	1 tbsp	1 tbsp	1 tbsp
Salt	pinch	pinch	pinch
Milk	275 ml	½ pt	1¼ cups
Plaice	450–700 g	1–1½ lb	1–1½ lb
Flour	2 tbsp	2 tbsp	2 tbsp
Salt and freshly ground black pepper			

For the sauce

Parsley	few sprigs	few sprigs	few sprigs
Egg yolks	2	2	2
Dry mustard	¼ tsp	¼ tsp	¼ tsp
Wine vinegar	5 ml	1 tsp	1 tsp
Salad oil	150 ml	¼ pt	⅔ cup
Egg, hard-boiled	1	1	1
Capers	1 tbsp	1 tbsp	1 tbsp
Gherkins	3	3	3

Blend the plain flour, egg yolk, oil and salt until smooth. Add the milk and blend. Whisk the egg white, add to the blender and blend just for a few seconds to mix in.

Skin the plaice and cut into strips. Season the flour and roll the strips of fish in it. Dip the fish in the batter and deep fry for 4–5 minutes until crisp. Drain.

Meanwhile, make the sauce. Chop the parsley in the blender. Remove. Place the egg yolks, mustard and wine vinegar in the blender. Blend. Whilst the blender is running, slowly add the oil, drop by drop, until all has been used.

Cut the hard-boiled egg into quarters and add to the blender along with the capers, gherkins and parsley and blend until they are finely chopped and mixed together.

Serve as a starter or lunch dish.

NOTE
Do not freeze.

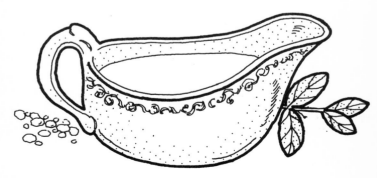

Codsteak Parcels with Baked Tomatoes

INGREDIENTS	Metric	Imperial	American
Mushrooms	*175 g*	*6 oz*	*6 oz*
Butter	*25 g*	*1 oz*	*2 tbsp*
Frozen codsteaks	*4*	*4*	*4*
Bacon	*4 slices*	*4 slices*	*4 slices*
Parsley	*few sprigs*	*few sprigs*	*few sprigs*
Salt and freshly ground black pepper			
Tomatoes	*4 med*	*4 med*	*4 med*
Butter	*25 g*	*1 oz*	*2 tbsp*
Castor sugar	*1 tsp*	*1 tsp*	*1 tsp*

Wash the mushrooms and chop roughly. Place in the blender and blend until finely chopped. You may have to do this in two batches. Add the butter, cut into pieces, and chop. Place the codsteaks, still frozen, on individual pieces of foil. Divide the mushroom mixture between them. Derind the bacon and chop finely. Spread on top of the mushrooms. Chop the parsley in the blender and sprinkle this on top. Season each codsteak. Fold over the foil to make a parcel then place in a deep ovenproof dish.

Cut the tomatoes in half, add a small knob of butter to each, plus a little sugar and salt and pepper. Place these in the dish. Cook at

200°C/400°F/Gas mark 6 for 35–40 minutes. Then open the parcels and cook for a further 5 minutes to crisp up the topping.

NOTE
Do not freeze.

Kipper and Tomato Flan

2 months

INGREDIENTS	Metric	Imperial	American
Wholemeal flour	75 g	3 oz	¾ cup
Plain flour	75 g	3 oz	¾ cup
Salt	pinch	pinch	pinch
Lard	25 g	1 oz	2 tbsp
Margarine	50 g	2 oz	¼ cup
Water	30–45 ml	2–3 tbsp	2–3 tbsp
Kippers	225 g	8 oz	½ lb
Chervil	few sprigs	few sprigs	few sprigs
Milk	150 ml	¼ pt	⅔ cup
Eggs	2	2	2
Salt and freshly ground black pepper			
Tomatoes	3	3	3

Place the flour in a large bowl. Add the salt and the fats, cut into pieces, and use the mixer to rub the fat into the flour until it resembles fine breadcrumbs. Add sufficient water to hold the pastry together, then roll out. Use to line a 20 cm/ 8 inch flan ring.

Skin the fish, break up and place in the pastry flan. Chop the chervil in the blender, add the milk and eggs, season well and blend until well combined. Pour over the fish. Thinly slice the tomatoes and arrange over the top of the flan.

Bake at 200°C/400°F/Gas mark 6 for 35 minutes until well risen, set and brown. Serve hot or warm.

TO FREEZE
Cool, then overwrap. Thaw for 6 hours at room temperature. Reheat for 15 minutes at 200°C/ 400°F/Gas mark 6.

VEGETABLES

Cauliflower Polenaise

INGREDIENTS	Metric	Imperial	American
Cauliflower	*1*	*1*	*1*
Garlic	*1 clove*	*1 clove*	*1 clove*
Butter	*50 g*	*2 oz*	*¼ cup*
Bread	*50 g*	*2 oz*	*2 slices*
Parsley	*few sprigs*	*few sprigs*	*few sprigs*
Hard-boiled egg	*1*	*1*	*1*

Wash the cauliflower and break into large florets.
Cook in boiling salted water for 8–10 minutes until
just soft. Drain and turn into a serving dish.

Meanwhile, crush the garlic clove and fry in the
butter. Break the bread into pieces, place in the
blender and make into breadcrumbs. Add to the
garlic and fry until lightly browned. Chop the
parsley in the blender, then add to pan. Cut the egg
into 4, place in the blender and blend until finely
chopped. Add to the pan, stir well and pour over
the cauliflower. Serve at once.

NOTE
Do not freeze.

Spinach Florentine

INGREDIENTS	Metric	Imperial	American
Spinach, fresh	*900 g*	*2 lb*	*2 lb*
OR *Frozen*	*450 g*	*1 lb*	*1 lb*
Melted butter	*25 g*	*1 oz*	*2 tbsp*
Milk	*425 ml*	*¾ pt*	*2 cups*
Butter	*40 g*	*1½ oz*	*3 tbsp*
Flour	*40 g*	*1½ oz*	*⅜ cup*
Salt and freshly ground black pepper			
Eggs	*4*	*4*	*4*

Wash the fresh spinach in several changes of water.
Cook in a very little boiling salted water for 7–8
minutes. Drain well. Purée in batches in the
blender, adding a little melted butter to each batch.
If using frozen spinach, defrost and heat in a pan,
then purée. Remove from the blender.

Place the milk, butter and flour in the blender.
Blend until well combined. Pour into a pan and
heat, stirring, until the sauce thickens. Season well.

Mix one third of the sauce with the spinach
purée and taste, adding more freshly ground pepper
if needed. Pour into an ovenproof dish. Make four
wells in the spinach mixture and break an egg into
each one. Cover with the remaining sauce. Cook at
190°C/375°F/Gas mark 5 for 20–30 minutes.

Serve hot as a starter or lunch dish.

NOTE
Do not freeze.

Tomatoes Duxelle

INGREDIENTS

	Metric	Imperial	American
Tomatoes	4 large	4 large	4 large
Onion	1	1	1
Butter	25 g	1 oz	2 tbsp
Mushrooms	50 g	2 oz	2 oz
Bread	25 g	1 oz	1 slice
Parsley or basil	few sprigs	few sprigs	few sprigs
Egg yolk	1	1	1
Salt and freshly ground black pepper			

Cut the stalk ends from the tomatoes and scoop out the seeds. Reserve the cut ends as lids. Chop the onion finely and fry in the butter. Add the finely chopped mushrooms and cook for 2–3 minutes.

Make the bread into crumbs in the blender, then add the herbs and blend again to chop them. Add this to the onion and mushroom mixture. Stir in the egg yolk and season well. Use to fill the tomato shells. Replace the lids and place in an ovenproof dish. Bake at 190°C/375°F/Gas mark 5 for 20–25 minutes.

Serve hot as a starter or lunch dish.

NOTE
Do not freeze.

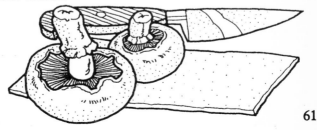

Stuffed Peppers

3 months

INGREDIENTS	Metric	Imperial	American
Red or green peppers	4 med	4 med	4 med
Leek	1	1	1
Oil	15 ml	1 tbsp	1 tbsp
Bacon	100 g	4 oz	1/4 lb
Mushrooms	50 g	2 oz	2 oz
Sweetcorn or frozen mixed vegetables	100 g	4 oz	1/4 lb
Butter	15 g	1/2 oz	1 tbsp
Flour	15 g	1/2 oz	2 tbsp
Milk	275 ml	1/2 pt	1 1/4 cups
Dry English mustard	1/2 tsp	1/2 tsp	1/2 tsp
Salt and freshly ground black pepper			
Lancashire or other crumbly cheese	50 g	2 oz	2 oz

Cut the peppers in half lengthwise and remove the seed. Wash the leek, trim and slice and fry in the oil until soft and brown. Derind and chop the bacon and fry with the leek. Wash and chop the mushrooms and fry until soft. Add the sweetcorn or vegetables.

Place the butter, flour, milk and mustard in the blender and blend until well combined. Pour into a saucepan and bring to the boil, stirring continuously. Once thickened, return to the blender. Season well, and add the cheese cut into cubes. Blend until the cheese is well mixed in. Add the cooked bacon and vegetables to the sauce and use to fill the pepper halves. Place in a shallow ovenproof dish, cover with foil and bake at 200°C/400°F/Gas mark 6 for 30 minutes. Remove the foil and bake for a further 5–10 minutes until brown.

TO FREEZE
Allow to cool. Pack into freezer bags or a box. Thaw for 5–6 hours at room temperature. Reheat for 15–20 minutes at 200°C/400°F/Gas mark 6.

Sweetcorn Fritters

INGREDIENTS	Metric	Imperial	American
Bread	*50 g*	*2 oz*	*2 slices*
Sweetcorn, frozen	*225 g*	*8 oz*	*½ lb*
Eggs	*2*	*2*	*2*
Salt and freshly ground black pepper			
Baking powder	*1 tsp*	*1 tsp*	*1 tsp*
Oil for frying			

Make the bread into crumbs in the blender. Thaw the sweetcorn. Separate the eggs, and beat the yolks with plenty of salt and pepper. Add the sweetcorn and baking powder. Whisk the egg whites with the mixer until stiff. Fold into the egg and sweetcorn mixture along with the breadcrumbs. Fry spoonfuls of the mixture in hot shallow oil. Turn once during cooking.

Serve hot with chicken dishes.

NOTE
Do not freeze.

Nut and Vegetable Medley

2 months

INGREDIENTS	Metric	Imperial	American
Aubergine	1	1	1
Leeks	2	2	2
Oil	15 ml	1 tbsp	1 tbsp
Potato	1 large	1 large	1 large
Mushrooms	50 g	2 oz	2 oz
Cabbage	½ small	½ small	½ small
Bread	50 g	2 oz	2 slices
Cashews	50 g	2 oz	2 oz
Butter	25 g	1 oz	2 tbsp
Salt and freshly ground black pepper			
Tinned tomatoes	400 g	14 oz	med tin
Paprika	1 tsp	1 tsp	1 tsp
Smoked cheese	75 g	3 oz	3 oz

Slice the aubergine, lay it on a flat plate, sprinkle with salt, cover and leave for 30 minutes. Wash and trim the leeks, slice and fry in the oil. Peel and slice the potato and put a layer into the base of an ovenproof dish. Add the leeks. Slice the mushrooms and add to the dish. Slice the cabbage and add. Drain the aubergine and place on top.

Make the bread into crumbs in the blender, add the cashews and blend until chopped. Add the butter, in pieces. Blend, and season. Remove.

Blend the tin of tomatoes with the paprika and pour over the vegetables. Cut the cheese into slices and arrange over the vegetables. Sprinkle the breadcrumb mixture on top. Cover and bake for 1–1½ hours at 180°C/350°F/Gas mark 4.

TO FREEZE
Cook, then pack into a freezer container. Thaw for
6–8 hours at room temperature. Reheat at
200°C/400°F/Gas mark 6 for 20–30 minutes.

Baked Potatoes with Chick Peas

INGREDIENTS	Metric	Imperial	American
Chick peas, tinned	100 g	4 oz	¼ lb
OR Dried	50 g	2 oz	2 oz
Potatoes	4 large	4 large	4 large
Butter	50 g	2 oz	¼ cup
Salt and freshly ground black pepper			
Grated cheese	100 g	2 oz	2 oz

If using dried chick peas, soak and cook as directed
on the packet.

Wash the potatoes, prick all over with a fork and
bake at 200°C/400°F/Gas mark 6 for 50–60 minutes
until soft.

Purée the chick peas in the blender, in batches if
necessary. Scrape down as needed.

Cut the potato in half, scoop out the flesh and
mash using the mixer. Add the butter, cut into
pieces, and the chick peas and mix well. Season
well, and pile back into the potato shells. Sprinkle
grated cheese on top of each potato half and return
to the oven for 10 minutes to brown.

NOTE
Do not freeze.

Broccoli with Hollandaise Sauce

INGREDIENTS	Metric	Imperial	American
Broccoli	*450 g*	*1 lb*	*1 lb*
Wine vinegar	*10 ml*	*2 tsp*	*2 tsp*
Lemon juice	*20 ml*	*4 tsp*	*4 tsp*
Butter	*100 g*	*4 oz*	*½ cup*
Egg yolks	*2*	*2*	*2*
Salt	*pinch*	*pinch*	*pinch*
Castor sugar	*pinch*	*pinch*	*pinch*

Wash the broccoli and cook in a little boiling salted water for 7–8 minutes.

Place the wine vinegar and lemon juice in a pan and bring to the boil. Melt the butter in another pan. Place the egg yolks, salt and castor sugar in the blender and blend. Pour on the vinegar and lemon juice and blend for 5–10 seconds. With the blender running, pour the melted butter in through the lid. Begin very gradually and only increase the flow as the sauce thickens. Once all the butter has been incorporated, scrape down and blend again.

Drain the broccoli, place on a warm serving dish and pour the sauce over.

NOTE
Do not freeze.

SAUCES AND STUFFINGS

Sauces can transform any dish — meat, pasta or salad. Use your blender to take the hard work out of sauce-making. Use the basic guides for how to make successful mayonnaise and white sauce and experiment with the more unusual recipes.

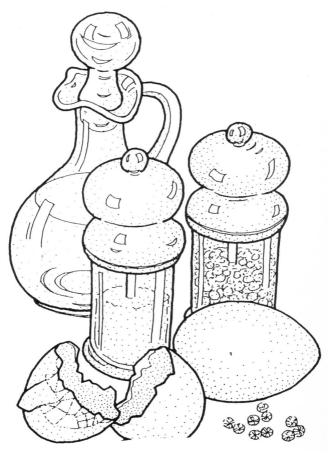

Mayonnaise

Use the blender to take the hard work out of home-made mayonnaise. Have all ingredients at room temperature and be patient. Add the oil very gradually at first for best results. Always choose a good light salad oil such as safflower oil, or olive oil for a stronger flavour, or mix the two.

INGREDIENTS	Metric	Imperial	American
Egg yolks	3	3	3
English mustard	½ tsp	½ tsp	½ tsp
Salt and freshly ground black pepper			
Wine vinegar	15 ml	1 tbsp	1 tbsp
Salad oil	275 ml	½ pt	1¼ cups

1. Place the egg yolks in the blender and add the mustard, seasonings, and 5 ml/1 tsp of the wine vinegar.
2. With the motor running, gradually add the oil through the hole in the lid. Start with a very thin trickle, and only increase the speed as the mayonnaise begins to combine. The sound of the blender will change as the mayonnaise thickens. Once this change in pitch is heard the oil can be added more quickly. Finally add the remaining vinegar, adjust the seasoning and blend again to incorporate.
3. Turn out the mayonnaise. If it looks very slightly curdled once made, add 15 ml/1 tbsp of hot water to the mayonnaise in the blender and blend briefly.

Parsley and Cheese Sauce

Blend the ingredients for a white sauce before cooking so that the flour and butter are well combined and the sauce can be made in one step. Sauces that have been frozen and begun to separate can also be blended briefly to make them smooth and creamy before reheating.

INGREDIENTS	Metric	Imperial	American
Parsley	*few sprigs*	*few sprigs*	*few sprigs*
Milk	*425 ml*	*¾ pt*	*2 cups*
Butter	*25 g*	*1 oz*	*2 tbsp*
Flour	*25 g*	*1 oz*	*¼ cup*
Salt and freshly ground black pepper			
Cheese	*50 g*	*2 oz*	*2 oz*

1. Wash the parsley, dry and chop finely in the blender by dropping it onto the revolving blades.
2. Without removing the parsley, add the milk, then the butter, cut into pieces, and the flour.
3. Blend for 10–15 seconds until the fat is cut into small pieces and the flour combined with the milk.
4. Pour into a pan and heat, stirring all the time until the sauce thickens. Season well.
5. Once the sauce is thick enough to coat the back of a wooden spoon, return it to the blender.
6. Add the cheese, cut into cubes, to the still-hot sauce, and then blend again until the cheese is well combined with the sauce. A good crumbly English cheese such as Lancashire works best and gives a tangy flavour.

French Dressing

INGREDIENTS	Metric	Imperial	American
Parsley	few sprigs	few sprigs	few sprigs
Wine vinegar	45 ml	3 tbsp	3 tbsp
Good salad oil	90 ml	6 tbsp	6 tbsp
French mustard	½ tsp	½ tsp	½ tsp
Castor sugar	½ tsp	½ tsp	½ tsp
Salt and freshly ground black pepper			

Chop the parsley in the blender. Add the other ingredients and blend until well combined and thick.

NOTE
Do not freeze.

Yoghurt and Chive Dressing

INGREDIENTS	Metric	Imperial	American
Chives	10–12 sprigs	10–12 sprigs	10–12 sprigs
Natural yoghurt	150 ml	¼ pt	⅔ cup
Wine vinegar	15 ml	1 tbsp	1 tbsp
Castor sugar	½ tsp	½ tsp	½ tsp
Spring onions	2	2	2
Salt and freshly ground black pepper			

Chop the chives in the blender. Add the yoghurt, wine vinegar and castor sugar and blend. Chop the spring onions and add. Season well and blend again.

Use as a salad dressing.

NOTE
Do not freeze.

Soubise Sauce

INGREDIENTS	Metric	Imperial	American
Onion	*1 large*	*1 large*	*1 large*
Water	*150 ml*	*¼ pt*	*⅔ cup*
Milk	*275 ml*	*½ pt*	*1¼ cups*
Butter or margarine	*25 g*	*1 oz*	*2 tbsp*
Flour	*25 g*	*1 oz*	*¼ cup*
Salt and freshly ground black pepper			

Peel the onion and cut into 4. Place in a pan with the water and cook gently until tender. Place the onion and water in the blender and blend until smooth. Add the milk, butter or margarine, cut into pieces, flour and salt and pepper. Blend until well combined. Pour into a pan and heat, stirring, until thickened. Check the seasoning. Serve hot.

TO FREEZE
Cool, then pour into a container and freeze. Thaw for 3–4 hours, then pour into the blender and blend for a few seconds. Reheat gently, stirring well.

Basil and Tomato Sauce

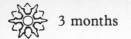 3 months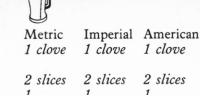

INGREDIENTS	Metric	Imperial	American
Garlic	*1 clove*	*1 clove*	*1 clove*
Oil for frying			
Streaky bacon	*2 slices*	*2 slices*	*2 slices*
Onion	*1*	*1*	*1*
Basil, fresh	*few sprigs*	*few sprigs*	*few sprigs*
OR *Dried*	*1 tsp*	*1 tsp*	*1 tsp*
Tinned tomatoes	*100 g*	*14 oz*	*med can*

Crush the garlic and fry in the oil until brown. Add the chopped bacon and onion and fry for 3–4 minutes.

Place the basil in the blender and chop finely. Add the tomatoes. Blend together. Add the onion and bacon and blend until smooth. Place in a pan to reheat.

Serve with pasta or meat.

TO FREEZE
Pour into a freezer container. Thaw for 3–4 hours at room temperature. Blend for a few seconds before reheating in a saucepan for 5–10 minutes.

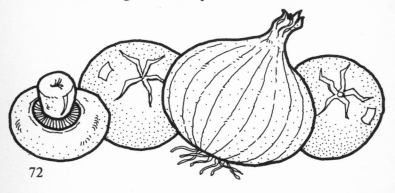

Bread Sauce

INGREDIENTS	Metric	Imperial	American
Milk	*275 ml*	*½ pt*	*1¼ cups*
Onion	*1 small*	*1 small*	*1 small*
Bay leaf	*1*	*1*	*1*
Cloves	*2*	*2*	*2*
White bread	*40 g*	*1½ oz*	*1½ slices*
Butter	*15 g*	*½ oz*	*1 tbsp*
Freshly ground black pepper			

Warm the milk. Add the onion, cut in half, the bay leaf and the cloves and leave to infuse for 20–30 minutes. Make the bread into crumbs in the blender. Strain the milk to remove the onion and flavourings. Bring the milk to the boil, add the crumbs, and then beat in the butter, cut into pieces. Season well with pepper and set aside to cool.

Serve cold with roast poultry or game.

NOTE
Do not freeze.

Orange Mint Sauce

INGREDIENTS	Metric	Imperial	American
Fresh mint	*small bunch*	*small bunch*	*small bunch*
Boiling water	*1 tbsp*	*1 tbsp*	*1 tbsp*
Castor sugar	*2–3 tsp*	*2–3 tsp*	*2–3 tsp*
Wine vinegar	*30 ml*	*2 tbsp*	*2 tbsp*
Orange juice	*60 ml*	*4 tbsp*	*4 tbsp*

Wash the mint, then chop in the blender. Add the boiling water and sugar and blend. Then add the wine vinegar and orange juice and blend again.

Serve with lamb and other meats.

NOTE
Do not freeze.

Bechamel Sauce

 2 months

INGREDIENTS	Metric	Imperial	American
Onion	*1 small*	*1 small*	*1 small*
Peppercorns	*6*	*6*	*6*
Bay leaf	*1*	*1*	*1*
Milk	*425 ml*	*¾ pt*	*2 cups*
Butter or margarine	*25 g*	*1 oz*	*2 tbsp*
Flour	*25 g*	*1 oz*	*¼ cup*
Salt and freshly ground black pepper			

Peel the onion and cut it in half. Place the onion, peppercorns and bay leaf in the milk. Warm the milk, then leave to stand for 20–30 minutes so the flavours can infuse. Strain the milk into the blender, add the butter or margarine, cut into pieces, and the flour, salt and pepper. Blend until well combined. Pour back into the pan and heat, stirring constantly, until the sauce thickens.

TO FREEZE
Cool, then pour into a container and freeze. Thaw for 3–4 hours at room temperature. Return to the blender, blend for a few seconds and then reheat in a pan.

Tomato and Pepper Stuffing

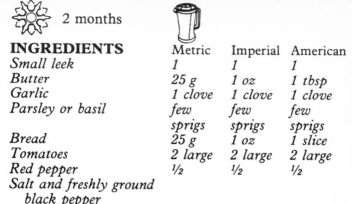

2 months

INGREDIENTS	Metric	Imperial	American
Small leek	1	1	1
Butter	25 g	1 oz	1 tbsp
Garlic	1 clove	1 clove	1 clove
Parsley or basil	few sprigs	few sprigs	few sprigs
Bread	25 g	1 oz	1 slice
Tomatoes	2 large	2 large	2 large
Red pepper	½	½	½
Salt and freshly ground black pepper			

Wash and trim the leek, slice and fry in the butter. Add the crushed garlic and fry until brown. Chop the herbs in the blender, add the bread and make into crumbs. Chop the tomatoes. Deseed and chop the red pepper, then blanch in boiling water for 2 minutes and drain. Mix together all the vegetables and the breadcrumb mixture and season well.

Use to stuff meat and poultry.

TO FREEZE
Make up as directed, pack into a small freezer box and freeze. Thaw for 1-2 hours at room temperature before using.

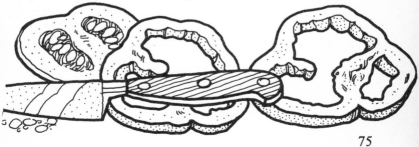

Kidney and Mushroom Stuffing

 1 month

INGREDIENTS	Metric	Imperial	American
Pistachio nuts	25 g	1 oz	1 oz
Lamb kidney	225 g	8 oz	½ lb
Butter	25 g	1 oz	2 tbsp
Mushrooms	50 g	2 oz	2 oz
Long grain rice, cooked	50 g	2 oz	2 oz
Thyme	½ tsp	½ tsp	½ tsp
Rosemary	½ tsp	½ tsp	½ tsp

Chop the nuts in the blender. Remove. Cut up the kidneys and fry in the butter. When they are just soft, place in the blender and chop roughly. Return to the pan. Add the mushrooms and cook for a few minutes. Then add the rice, nuts and herbs. Stir well.

Use to stuff meat and poultry.

TO FREEZE
Pack into a freezer box. Thaw for 4–5 hours at room temperature. Use as required.

Rich Custard Sauce

INGREDIENTS	Metric	Imperial	American
Egg yolks	2	2	2
Custard powder	25 g	1 oz	2 tbsp
Castor sugar	25 g	1 oz	2 tbsp
Milk	575 ml	1 pt	2½ cups

Place the egg yolks, custard powder, castor sugar and two tablespoons of the milk in the blender. Blend until smooth. Heat the remaining milk, bring to the boil and then pour onto the egg mixture in the blender all at once. Replace the lid and blend for 30 seconds until light and thick. Serve hot.

For trifles and other dishes where a thick custard is required, reduce the milk to 425 ml/¾ pt/2 cups.

NOTE
Do not freeze.

Fluffy Almond Sauce

 3 months

INGREDIENTS	Metric	Imperial	American
Almonds	25 g	1 oz	1 oz
Milk	575 ml	1 pt	2½ cups
Flour	1 tbsp	1 tbsp	1 tbsp
Castor sugar	1 tbsp	1 tbsp	1 tbsp
Egg	1	1	1

Grind the almonds in the blender until finely chopped. Add the milk, flour, sugar and the egg yolk. Blend for a few seconds until smooth. Pour into a pan and bring to the boil, stirring all the time until thick. Allow to cool slightly, then return to the blender and blend for about 10 seconds. Use the mixer to whisk the egg white, then add it to the blender. Blend just long enough to incorporate the egg white.

Serve warm.

TO FREEZE
Pour into a freezer container. Thaw for 2–3 hours at room temperature. Reheat gently in a pan.

Sauce Cassis

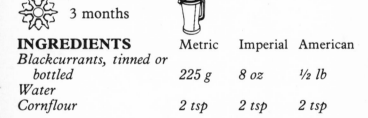 3 months

INGREDIENTS	Metric	Imperial	American
Blackcurrants, tinned or			
bottled	225 g	8 oz	½ lb
Water			
Cornflour	2 tsp	2 tsp	2 tsp

Purée the fruit in the blender. Make up to 425 ml/ ¾ pint/2 cups with water.

Mix 1 tbsp of the purée with the cornflour. Heat the remainder. Add to the cornflour. Stir well. Return to the pan and bring to the boil, stirring all the time.

Serve warm or pour over fruit and allow to set.

TO FREEZE
Allow to cool, then pour into a freezer container. Thaw for 3–4 hours at room temperature.

DESSERTS

Fruit Fool

Fools can be made with any fresh soft fruits, or
with cooked fruits such as apples, rhubarb or
gooseberries. Use the blender to prepare both the
custard base and to purée the fruit, but whip the
cream separately for a light result.

INGREDIENTS	Metric	Imperial	American
Custard powder	25 g	1 oz	1 oz
Egg yolk	1	1	1
Milk	275 ml	½ pt	1 ¼ cups
Soft fruits e.g. raspberries or strawberries	350 g	12 oz	¾ lb
Castor sugar	50 g	2 oz	¼ cup
Double or whipping (heavy) cream	275 ml	½ pt	1 ¼ cups

1. To make the rich custard sauce, place the custard
   powder in the blender and add the egg yolk.
   Heat the milk and add to the egg yolk mixture. If
   the blender can withstand boiling liquids, add the
   milk just as it comes to the boil and the custard
   should thicken as you blend it. If the blender
   cannot take boiling liquids, add the milk while
   hot, blend and then return to the pan and bring
   to the boil, stirring, to thicken the custard. Allow
   to cool.
2. Place the soft fruit in the blender with the sugar.
   Reserve some whole fruits for decoration. Blend
   until puréed. Scrape down as necessary.

3. Whisk the cream in a bowl until it forms soft peaks.
4. Fold the puréed fruit into the cream, then fold in the cold custard mixture.
5. Pour into serving dishes. Decorate with reserved soft fruits and chill for 20 minutes before serving.

Peach Cream

INGREDIENTS	Metric	Imperial	American
Pudding rice	25 g	1 oz	1 oz
Milk	275 ml	½ pt	1¼ cups
Tinned peaches	400 g	14 oz	large tin
Gelatine	15 g	½ oz	1 sachet
Double (heavy) cream	275 ml	½ pt	1¼ cups

Put the rice and milk in a pan and cook until the rice is soft and thick.

Mix 45 ml/3 tbsp of the peach juice with the gelatine and dissolve over hot water.

Reserve some peach slices for decoration. Blend the remaining peaches and juice. Add the rice mixture and blend. Pour the gelatine in through the lid with the blender running.

Use the mixer to whip half the cream, then add this to the blender. Blend just enough to incorporate. Pour into a dish or mould and allow to set.

Decorate with the reserved peaches and remaining cream piped on top.

NOTE
Do not freeze.

Baked Stuffed Apples with Lemon Butter Sauce

 4 months

INGREDIENTS	Metric	Imperial	American
Cooking apples	*4*	*4*	*4*
Dates, stoned	*100 g*	*4 oz*	*¼ lb*
Golden syrup	*1 tbsp*	*1 tbsp*	*1 tbsp*
Butter	*15 g*	*½ oz*	*1 tbsp*
Demerara sugar	*2 tbsp*	*2 tbsp*	*2 tbsp*
Lemon	*1*	*1*	*1*
Water	*1 tbsp*	*1 tbsp*	*1 tbsp*
Cornflour	*1 tbsp*	*1 tbsp*	*1 tbsp*

Core the apples and score the skin all round. Chop the dates in the blender and use to stuff centre of the apples. Bake at 180°C/350°F/Gas mark 4 for 40–45 minutes.

Place the golden syrup, butter and demerara sugar in the blender. Squeeze the juice of the lemon, make up to 150 ml/¼ pt/⅓ cup with water and add to the blender. Sprinkle in the cornflour and then blend until smooth. Pour into a pan, bring to the boil, stirring constantly, then reduce the heat and simmer for 5–10 minutes. Serve with the baked apples.

TO FREEZE
Freeze the apples and sauce separately. Pack into freezer containers. Thaw for 6–7 hours at room temperature. Reheat the sauce in a pan. Reheat the apples at 200°C/400°F/Gas mark 6 for 15–20 minutes.

81

Meringue

Good meringues need thorough whisking of the egg whites and careful addition of the sugar. Always ensure that the bowl used is completely free from grease and that there are no traces of egg yolk in the mixture or this will prevent the whites from whisking properly.

INGREDIENTS	Metric	Imperial	American
Egg whites	*2*	*2*	*2*
Castor sugar	*100 g*	*4 oz*	*½ cup*

1. Place the egg whites in a large bowl.
2. Whisk steadily for several minutes until the whites stand in soft peaks.
3. You can check the stiffness of the whites by turning the bowl upside down. Once properly whisked they will remain in the bowl and not slide out!
4. Add half the castor sugar, and whisk again until the mixture looks glossy and will stand in peaks again.
5. Fold in the other half of the sugar using a metal spoon. Turn the bowl as you fold so that all the sugar is folded in.
6. Place the mixture in a piping bag and pipe into small stars or rosettes, or shape into a circle for a gateau. Use a non-stick baking tray or greased, greaseproof paper to make it easy to remove the meringues once cooked.

TO FREEZE: Meringues or Pavlova shells — open freeze, overwrap or place in freezer box. Thaw in fridge for 6-8 hours.

Hazelnut Pavlova

 2 months

INGREDIENTS

	Metric	Imperial	American
Hazelnuts	*75 g*	*3 oz*	*3 oz*
Egg whites	*3*	*3*	*3*
Castor sugar	*175 g*	*6 oz*	*¾ cup*
Wine vinegar	*few drops*	*few drops*	*few drops*
Whipping cream	*275 ml*	*½ pt*	*1¼ cups*
Soft fruit in season e.g. raspberries, strawberries, 2–3 sliced kiwi fruits or small tin mandarins, well drained	*225 g*	*8 oz*	*½ lb*

Chop the hazelnuts in the blender. You may need to do this in two batches. Whisk the egg whites using the mixer until they form soft peaks. Add half the sugar and whisk again until the mixture forms soft peaks. Fold in the remaining sugar, nuts and wine vinegar using a metal spoon. Line a baking tray with a piece of greased, greaseproof paper and pipe or spoon the meringue into a circle about 20 cm/8 ins in diameter. Pipe a circle of stars around the edge, or use a spoon to form some of the meringue into a raised edge. Bake at 190°C/375°F/Gas mark 5 for 15–20 minutes until brown and crisp on top. Turn the oven off, and leave with the door ajar until the meringue is cool.

Use the mixer to whisk the cream until stiff enough to pipe. Spread half the cream in the base of the pavlova and place the soft fruit on top. Finish with piped stars of cream around the edge. **Pavlova base may be stored for several days in an airtight tin.**

Biscuit Base

Uncooked biscuit flan bases go well with creamy, fruity fillings and are quick to make using the blender to prepare the biscuits. Use digestive or ginger biscuits, or for a change try using chocolate digestive biscuits.

INGREDIENTS	Metric	Imperial	American
Biscuits	*8*	*8*	*8*
Butter	*50 g*	*2 oz*	*4 tbsp*

1. Break the biscuits up roughly, and place them in the blender. If the feed hole is large enough, drop the biscuits onto the revolving blades. If not, put the biscuits into the blender first then switch on. Process in batches until all the biscuits are finely chopped.
2. Pour the biscuit crumbs onto the melted butter and mix well.
3. Tip out into a flan ring and press firmly against the sides and base. Chill for 30 minutes before filling.

Pineapple Ice Cream Pie

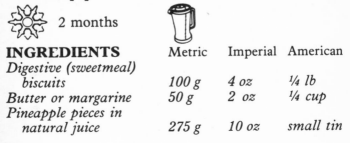

2 months

INGREDIENTS	Metric	Imperial	American
Digestive (sweetmeal) biscuits	*100 g*	*4 oz*	*¼ lb*
Butter or margarine	*50 g*	*2 oz*	*¼ cup*
Pineapple pieces in natural juice	*275 g*	*10 oz*	*small tin*

Cornflour	1 tsp	1 tsp	1 tsp
Lemon	½	½	½
Honey	1 tsp	1 tsp	1 tsp
Soft scoop ice cream	1 l	1¾ pt	4⅓ cups
Almonds	25 g	1 oz	1 oz

Break up the biscuits, then crush them in blender
in batches. Add the melted butter or margarine and
press into a 20 cm/8 inch flan ring. Place in the
fridge.

Drain the juice from the tin of pineapple.
Blend the cornflour with a little of the juice, then
heat the rest of the juice with the juice of ½ lemon
and 1 tsp of honey. Add the hot liquid to the
cornflour mixture and return to the pan over a low
heat to thicken. Allow to cool. Reserve a few pieces
for decorations, then purée the remaining pineapple
pieces in the blender and add to the sauce.

Place scoops of the ice cream in the biscuit
base, arranging them round and into a pyramid
shape. Pour the pineapple sauce over the ice cream.
Place in the freezer for 20–30 minutes. Remove,
sprinkle with nuts and decorate with the reserved
pineapple pieces. Serve immediately.

TO FREEZE
Open freeze until hard before decorating, then
cover. Thaw for 1–2 hours in the fridge before
serving. Add the nuts and pineapple pieces just
before serving.

Cooked Apricot Cheesecake

2-3 months

INGREDIENTS	Metric	Imperial	American
For the pastry			
Hazelnuts	25 g	1 oz	1 oz
Butter or margarine	75 g	3 oz	1/3 cup
Plain flour	100 g	4 oz	1 cup
Castor sugar	50 g	2 oz	1/4 cup
Cold water	30–45 ml	2–3 tbsp	2–3 tbsp
For the filling			
Dried apricots	100 g	4 oz	1/4 lb
Lemon	1	1	1
Curd cheese	100 g	4 oz	1/4 lb
Cream cheese	100 g	4 oz	1/4 lb
Castor sugar	50 g	2 oz	1/4 cup
Cornflour	25 g	1 oz	1 tbsp
Eggs	2	2	2
Icing sugar			

Wash the apricots for the filling and soak according to the instructions on the packet.

To make the pastry, grind the hazelnuts in the blender until finely chopped. Rub the butter or margarine into the flour until the mixture resembles fine breadcrumbs. Add the sugar and hazelnuts. Add sufficient cold water to make a firm pastry. Roll out and use to line an 18 cm/7 inch loose-bottomed flan ring.

Chop the apricots roughly in the blender. Remove, Place the grated rind and the juice of the lemon in the blender. Add the curd cheese and the cream cheese, cut into pieces. Blend. Scrape down and blend as necessary until the mixture is roughly combined. Add the sugar, cornflour and egg yolks. Blend until smooth and creamy.

Whisk the egg whites in a bowl and when stiff add the cream mixture and fold in. Spread the chopped apricots over the base of the flan, and pour the mixture on top. Bake in the oven at 180°C/350°F/Gas mark 4, for 30–40 minutes until well risen and golden brown. Allow to cool slightly then sieve a little icing sugar over the top. Serve warm or cold.

TO FREEZE
Open freeze until hard, then overwrap. Thaw at room temperature for 6 hours.

Ginger and Lemon Cheesecake

 2 months

INGREDIENTS	Metric	Imperial	American
Gingernut biscuits	175 g	6 oz	6 oz
Butter or margarine	50 g	2 oz	¼ cup
Gelatine	15 g	½ oz	1 sachet
Water	30 ml	2 tbsp	2 tbsp
Lemons	2	2	2
Cottage cheese	100 g	4 oz	¼ lb
Cream cheese	100 g	4 oz	¼ lb
Castor sugar	50 g	2 oz	¼ cup
Natural yoghurt	150 ml	¼ pt	⅔ cup
Double (heavy) cream	150 ml	¼ pt	⅔ cup

Break up the biscuits and chop finely in the blender in 2 or 3 batches. Tip into a bowl. Melt the butter and add to the biscuit crumbs. Stir well then press into the base of a 20 cm/8 inch flan ring. Chill.

Place the gelatine in a small bowl with 30 ml/
2 tbsp of water and stand in a pan of water. Heat
gently until the gelatine dissolves.

Use a potato peeler to thinly pare 2–3 strips of
lemon rind from one lemon. Grate the remaining
rind of both lemons. Cut the lemons into quarters,
remove the pips and skin and place the flesh in the
blender. Blend for 10–15 seconds until puréed. Add
the cottage cheese and the cream cheese, cut into
pieces. Blend for 5–10 seconds until all is mixed
together. Add the castor sugar, yoghurt and cream.
Blend again. Pour in the gelatine mixture and
blend. Pour into the biscuit flan base and leave in
the fridge to set for 1 hour. Decorate with lemon
rind cut into thin strips and extra cream if required.

TO FREEZE
Open freeze until hard. Wrap. Thaw in the fridge
overnight or for 2–3 hours at room temperature.

Apricot and Orange Pancakes

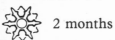 2 months

INGREDIENTS	Metric	Imperial	American
Dried apricots	50 g	2 oz	2 oz
Almonds	25 g	1 oz	1 oz
Plain flour	100 g	4 oz	1 cup
Salt	pinch	pinch	pinch
Egg	1	1	1
Milk	275 ml	½ pt	1¼ cups
Grated rind of orange	1	1	1

Melted butter	2 tbsp	2 tbsp	2 tbsp
Small oranges	2	2	2
Oil for frying			

Soak the apricots overnight.

Chop the almonds roughly in the blender. Remove. Place the flour, salt, egg and milk in the blender. Add the grated orange rind and melted butter and blend until well combined. Add the almonds and blend to incorporte.

Use this batter to make 6–8 pancakes. As each pancake is cooked, place it in a stack with sheets of greaseproof between each one.

Remove all the white pith from the 2 oranges and cut out the flesh. Chop the apricots in the blender and add the flesh of the oranges. Purée. Use to fill the pancakes. Roll up and place in a shallow dish. Cover with foil and reheat at 200°C/400°F/Gas mark 6 for 15–20 minutes.

Serve hot with cream.

TO FREEZE

Stuff the pancakes with the filling, place in a freezer container and freeze. Thaw for 6–7 hours at room temperature, then reheat as above.

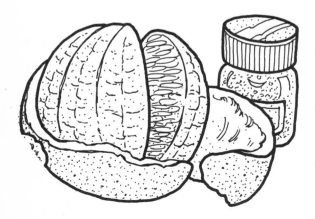

Apple Betty

 3-4 months

INGREDIENTS	Metric	Imperial	American
Cooking apples	700 g	1½ lb	1½ lb
Water	30 ml	2 tbsp	2 tbsp
Wholemeal bread	100 g	4 oz	4 slices
Walnuts	50 g	2 oz	2 oz
Lemon	1	1	1
Orange	1	1	1
Sultanas	25 g	1 oz	2 tbsp
Brown sugar	100 g	4 oz	½ cup
Butter	25 g	1 oz	2 tbsp
Cinnamon	½ tsp	½ tsp	½ tsp

Peel and core the apples, cut into thin slices and cook over a gentle heat in the water for 10 minutes until just soft. Make the bread into crumbs in the blender, remove, and chop the walnuts in the blender. Remove. Grate the rind from the lemon. Cut the lemon and the orange into quarters and remove the flesh, taking care not to include any white pith, which is bitter. Blend the segments until well mixed. Add the sultanas, half the brown sugar and lemon rind and blend to mix. Add the apple.

Place half of this mixture in the base of a deep dish. Sprinkle half the breadcrumbs and nuts and half the remaining sugar on top. Then add the rest of the apple mixture and the remaining breadcrumbs, nuts and finally the sugar on top. Cut the butter into small pieces and spread on top. Sprinkle with the cinnamon.

Bake at 190°C/375°F/Gas mark 5 for 30-40 minutes until crisp on the top. Serve hot with cream or custard.

TO FREEZE
Cool and overwrap. Thaw for 4–5 hours at room temperature. Reheat at 200°C/400°F/Gas mark 6 for 20 minutes.

Fluffy Apple Pudding

INGREDIENTS	Metric	Imperial	American
Milk	575 ml	1 pt	2½ cups
White bread	100 g	4 oz	4 slices
Butter	25 g	1 oz	2 tbsp
Lemon	1	1	1
Castor sugar	25 g	1 oz	2 tbsp
Eggs	2	2	2
Cooking apple	1 large	1 large	1 large
Brown sugar	1 tbsp	1 tbsp	1 tbsp

Heat the milk in a pan. Make the bread into crumbs in the blender and add to the hot milk. Add half the butter, the grated rind of the lemon and the castor sugar. Leave to stand for 15-20 minutes until most of the milk is absorbed.

Separate the eggs, add the yolks to the milk mixture and beat well. Whisk the egg whites and fold into the milk mixture.

Peel, core and slice the cooking apple. Use the remaining butter to grease a shallow dish. Place the apple slices in the dish, sprinkle the brown sugar on top and then pour the milk and breadcrumb mixture on top. Bake at 180°C/350°F/Gas mark 4 for 30 minutes until well risen and golden brown.

Serve hot.

NOTE
Do not freeze.

Date and Lemon Pudding

INGREDIENTS	Metric	Imperial	American
Dates, stoned	100 g	4 oz	¼ lb
Bread	25 g	1 oz	1 slice
Lemons	2	2	2
Water	75 g	3 oz	⅓ cup
Castor sugar	75 g	3 oz	⅓ cup
Soft (tub) margarine	100 g	4 oz	½ cup
Self-raising flour	100 g	4 oz	1 cup
Brown sugar	50 g	2 oz	¼ cup
Eggs	2	2	2

Place the dates in the blender and chop roughly. Remove. Break the bread into pieces, place in the blender and make into breadcrumbs. Remove. Grate the rinds of the lemons, cut into quarters and remove the flesh. Pick out the pips, then put the flesh in the blender and purée. Make up to 275 ml/½ pt/1¼ cups with water, add the castor sugar and place in a pan. Heat gently until the sugar is dissolved, then boil rapidly for a few minutes.

Meanwhile place the soft margarine, flour, brown sugar, eggs, breadcrumbs and lemon rind in a large bowl and mix until smooth. Add the chopped dates and mix in well. Turn into a well buttered 1 1/2 pt pudding basin. Pour the sauce over, then cover with pleated foil. Secure the top and steam for 1½–2 hours until the top is dry and spongy. Turn out with care as the sauce will pour round the pudding.

NOTE
Do not freeze.

TEATIME TREATS

All-in-one Victoria Sandwich Cake

All-in-one cake mixes are quick and easy to make. Ensure that the margarine is at room temperature. Soft margarines give the best result.

INGREDIENTS	Metric	Imperial	American
Eggs	*3*	*3*	*3*
Castor sugar	*175 g*	*6 oz*	*¾ cup*
Self-raising flour	*175 g*	*6 oz*	*1½ cups*
Soft margarine	*175 g*	*6 oz*	*¾ cup*
Baking powder	*1 tsp*	*1 tsp*	*1 tsp*

1. Place all ingredients in a large bowl.
2. Mix, using the hand mixer, until smooth.
3. Turn into cake tins and bake as usual. This mixture can also be used as a base for flavoured cakes and small buns.

VARIATIONS:

Chocolate sponge: Add 1½ oz of cocoa powder to the basic ingredients.

Orange or lemon sponge: Add grated rind of large orange or lemon and 1 tablespoon of the juice to the basic ingredients.

Orange Fruit Cake

3 months

INGREDIENTS

	Metric	Imperial	American
Orange	1	1	1
Mixed fruit	50 g	2 oz	2 oz
Glacé cherries	50 g	2 oz	2 oz
Self-raising flour	225 g	8 oz	2 cups
Baking powder	1 tsp	1 tsp	1 tsp
Soft brown sugar	100 g	4 oz	½ cup
Soft (tub) margarine	100 g	4 oz	½ cup
Eggs	2	2	2
Demerara sugar	1 tbsp	1 tbsp	1 tbsp

Grate the rind from the orange and squeeze the juice. Wash the fruit and the cherries. Cut the cherries into quarters. Soak the fruit in the orange juice for 1 hour.

Reserve 2 tablespoons of the flour. Place the rest in a large mixing bowl and add the baking powder, sugar, margarine, eggs and grated orange rind. Use the mixer to beat until smooth. Drain any juice from the fruit into the cake mixture; beat again with the mixer.

Add the 2 tablespoons of flour to the fruit and stir well so that the fruit is coated with flour. Fold the fruit into the cake using a metal spoon. Turn into a deep 20 cm/8 inch diameter cake tin, sprinkle with demerara sugar and bake at 180°C/350°F/Gas mark 4 for 40–60 minutes. Allow to cool slightly before turning out of the tin.

TO FREEZE
Wrap in foil or place in a polythene bag. Thaw for 4 hours at room temperature.

Coffee and Walnut Cake

3 months

INGREDIENTS	Metric	Imperial	American
Walnuts	*100 g*	*4 oz*	*¼ lb*
Self-raising flour	*100 g*	*4 oz*	*1 cup*
Eggs	*4*	*4*	*4*
Castor sugar	*100 g*	*4 oz*	*½ cup*
For the icing			
Icing sugar	*50 g*	*2 oz*	*¼ cup*
Egg white	*1*	*1*	*1*
Unsalted butter	*100 g*	*4 oz*	*½ cup*
Instant coffee	*1 tsp*	*1 tsp*	*1 tsp*
Boiling water	*5 ml*	*1 tsp*	*1 tsp*

Reserve some nuts for decoration. Finely chop the remaining nuts in the blender. You may need to do this in batches. Sieve the flour into a bowl and stand in a warm place. Place the eggs and castor sugar in a large bowl and stand the bowl over a pan of hot water. Make sure the water does not touch the base of the bowl. Whisk until light and frothy and thick enough to leave a trail. Remove from the heat and sieve the flour into the bowl. Add the nuts and carefully fold in the dry ingredients. Use a metal spoon and turn the bowl as you work, so that the spoon scrapes up any dry flour from the base of the bowl. Pour into a deep loose-based cake tin and bake at 190°C/375°F/Gas mark 5 for 20 minutes until brown. Remove and cool.

To make the icing, place the icing sugar and egg white in a large bowl and place over a pan of hot water. Whisk using the mixer until it becomes thick and very glossy. This may take 5–10 minutes. The mixture should stand in soft peaks when ready.

Remove from the heat. Cut the butter into pieces and beat these, one at a time, into the icing. Once all the butter is included, mix the coffee with the boiling water and stir this into the icing.

Chill for 30 minutes and then use to ice the sides and top of the cake. Decorate with walnut halves.

TO FREEZE
Open freeze until hard, then overwrap. Thaw for 4–5 hours at room temperature.

Bakewell Fingers

5 months

INGREDIENTS	Metric	Imperial	American
Almonds	50 g	2 oz	2 oz
Plain flour	175 g	6 oz	1½ cups
Margarine	50 g	2 oz	¼ cup
Lard	25 g	1 oz	2 tbsp
Water	30-45 ml	2–3 tbsp	2-3 tbsp
Jam	1 tbsp	1 tbsp	1 tbsp
Self-raising flour	100 g	4 oz	1 cup
Castor sugar	100 g	4 oz	½ cup
Soft margarine	100 g	4 oz	½ cup
Eggs	2	2	2
Icing (confectioner's) sugar	25 g	1 oz	2 tbsp

Chop the almonds finely in the blender. Place the plain flour in a large bowl, add the margarine and lard cut into pieces, and mix with the mixer until the fats are well rubbed into the flour. Add the water and mix again. Pull the pastry together with the fingertips, and roll out to fit a swiss roll tin.

Line the tin with the pastry. Save the pastry trimmings for decoration. Spread the jam evenly over the pastry.

Place the almonds, self-raising flour, sugar, soft margarine and eggs in a bowl and mix with the mixer until smooth. Spread over the jam. Roll out the pastry trimmings and cut long strips. Twist these and lay over the top of the sponge mixture. Bake at 190°C/350°F/Gas mark 5 for 20–30 minutes until brown and spongy to the touch. Allow to cool slightly, then cut into 16 fingers. Leave to cool in the tin.

Mixing the icing sugar with sufficient water to make into a smooth paste. Pipe the icing in lines over the fingers, or trickle the icing from a teaspoon.

TO FREEZE
Open freeze until hard then pack into a freezer bag. Thaw for 1–2 hours at room temperature.

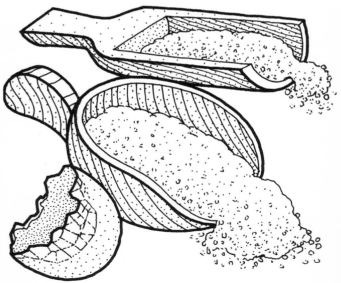

Almond Macaroons

 2 months

INGREDIENTS	Metric	Imperial	American
Almonds	100 g	4 oz	¼ lb
Castor sugar	175 g	6 oz	¾ cup
Egg whites	2	2	2
Vanilla essence	few drops	few drops	few drops

Reserve a few almonds, then grind the rest in the blender until finely chopped. Mix together the sugar and almonds. Whisk the egg whites until stiff and fold in the sugar and almonds and the vanilla essence. Once the mixture holds together, form into small balls and place on a baking tray lined with greased, greaseproof paper or rice paper. Flatten each ball slightly and place a split almond on top.

Bake at 180°C/350°F/Gas mark 4 for 15–20 minutes until golden brown around the edges but still slightly moist in the centre. Leave to cool and then remove from the greaseproof paper. If using rice paper, leave this on the biscuits.

Makes 16–20.

TO FREEZE
Place in a freezer box. Thaw for 2 hours at room temperature.

Fruity Flapjacks

 5 months

INGREDIENTS

	Metric	Imperial	American
Dates	225 g	8 oz	½ lb
Currants	50 g	2 oz	2 oz
Lemon juice	15 ml	1 tbsp	1 tbsp
Hot water	30 ml	2 tbsp	2 tbsp
Margarine	175 g	6 oz	¾ cup
Golden syrup	1 tbsp	1 tbsp	1 tbsp
Brown sugar	50 g	2 oz	¼ cup
Rolled oats	225 g	8 oz	½ lb
Plain flour	50 g	2 oz	½ cup

Chop the dates in the blender in batches. Chop the currants in the blender. Mix the two, and add the lemon juice and hot water. Mix well.

Melt the margarine, golden syrup and brown sugar together in a pan. Add the rolled oats and flour and stir well. Spread two-thirds of the mixture on the base of a swiss roll tin. Distribute the date mixture on top then spread the remaining oat mixture over this. Press down well.

Bake at 180°C/350°F/Gas mark 4 for 20–25 minutes until lightly brown. Allow to cool slightly then mark into fingers and cool in the tin.

Makes 16.

TO FREEZE
Pack into a freezer bag. Thaw for 2–3 hours at room temperature.

Brownies

 3–4 months

INGREDIENTS	Metric	Imperial	American
Walnuts	*75 g*	*3 oz*	*3 oz*
Cocoa	*50 g*	*2 oz*	*½ cup*
Water	*75 ml*	*5 tbsp*	*5 tbsp*
Margarine	*75 g*	*3 oz*	*6 tbsp*
Eggs	*2*	*2*	*2*
Castor sugar	*225 g*	*8 oz*	*1 cup*
Plain flour	*75 g*	*3 oz*	*¾ cup*
Baking powder	*½ tsp*	*½ tsp*	*½ tsp*

Chop the walnuts in the blender until roughly chopped. Remove. Place the cocoa in the blender, add the water and blend until smooth. Place in a pan with the margarine and melt gently.

Whisk the eggs and sugar together with the mixer until light and frothy, then stir in the cocoa and margarine mixture. Fold in the flour, baking powder and nuts. Place in greased, lined cake tin 20 cm/8 ins square and bake at 180°C/350°F/Gas mark 4 for 30–40 minutes. Mark into squares and allow to cool slightly before removing from the tin.

Makes 15.

TO FREEZE
Pack in polythene bags. Thaw for 2–3 hours at room temperature.

Drop Scones

INGREDIENTS	Metric	Imperial	American
Milk	150 ml	¼ pt	⅔ cup
Plain flour	100 g	4 oz	1 cup
Salt	pinch	pinch	pinch
Baking powder	2 tsp	2 tsp	2 tsp
Castor sugar	1 tbsp	1 tbsp	1 tbsp
Melted butter	25 g	1 oz	2 tbsp
Egg	1	1	1
Oil for cooking	15 ml	1 tbsp	1 tbsp

Heat a griddle or heavy-based frying pan over a moderate heat. Place the milk in the blender then add the other ingredients, except the oil, and blend until smooth. Oil the pan lightly. Pour tablespoons of the sauce mixture onto the hot pan. Cook for 2–3 minutes. When the scones lose their glossy tops and small bubbles appear, turn them over and cook for a further 2–3 minutes. As the scones are cooked, remove and cover with a warm tea towel while the rest are cooking.

Serve warm with butter, honey, jam or golden syrup.

Makes 12.

NOTE
Do not freeze.

101

ICINGS AND TOPPINGS

Butter Icing

 4 months

INGREDIENTS	Metric	Imperial	American
Butter	*100 g*	*4 oz*	*½ cup*
Icing (confectioner's) sugar	*225 g*	*8 oz*	*1 cup*
Hot water	*5–10 ml*	*1–2 tsp*	*1–2 tsp*

Cut the butter into pieces and mix, using the mixer, until soft. Add the sugar and mix in well. Add the hot water and mix again to make the icing soft enough to spread or pipe.

Flavour with any of the following:

1 tbsp lemon or orange juice;

1 tbsp finely grated orange or lemon rind;

2 tsp instant coffee mixed with hot water;

1–2 tbsp cocoa powder mixed to a paste with 1–2 tbsp boiling water;

100 g/2 oz/ 8 squares cooking chocolate, melted.

TO FREEZE

Either on cakes or by itself, in which case pack into a plastic container. Thaw for 4–5 hours at room temperature. Mix well, using the mixer, and add another 5-10 ml/1-2 tsp of hot water if necessary to soften the icing.

Chocolate Frosting

INGREDIENTS

Ingredient	Metric	Imperial	American
Chocolate	25 g	1 oz	1 oz
Cream	30 ml	2 tbsp	2 tbsp
Icing sugar	75 g	3 oz	6 tbsp

Grate the chocolate into a bowl, add the cream, and place over a pan of hot water until all the chocolate has melted.

Add the sugar and whisk until all is incorported into the mixture.

Use whilst warm and allow to set.

NOTE
Can be frozen once spread on cakes etc.

Blender Cream

INGREDIENTS

Ingredient	Metric	Imperial	American
Milk	150 ml	¼ pt	2/3 cup
Unsalted butter	125 g	5 oz	½ cup + 2 tbsp

Place the milk in a pan. Cut the butter into pieces and add to the milk. Heat until the butter melts. Do not boil. Pour into the blender and blend well. Pour into a jug, cover and chill in the fridge for several hours or overnight before use. This cream will whip sufficiently for mousses and soufflés.

NOTE
Do not freeze.

Crème Patissière

 3 months

INGREDIENTS	Metric	Imperial	American
Milk	*425 ml*	*¾ pt*	*2 cups*
Flour	*25 g*	*1 oz*	*¼ cup*
Cornflour	*15 g*	*½ oz*	*1 tbsp*
Castor sugar	*50 g*	*2 oz*	*¼ cup*
Egg	*1*	*1*	*1*

Place the milk in the blender. Add the flour and cornflour, and half the castor sugar. Add the egg yolk and blend until smooth. Pour into a pan and heat, stirring, until the mixture thickens and boils. Beware of curdling; if this happens, remove from the heat, return to the blender, add an ice cube and blend until smooth. Once thickened, leave to cool. Whisk the egg white, add the remaining castor sugar and fold into the cream.

Use to fill flan cases, or in cakes and gateaux. This may be flavoured with liqueurs or with grated orange or lemon rind.

TO FREEZE
Pour into a freezer container. Thaw for 3–4 hours at room temperature. Use as required.

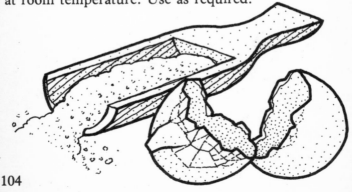

PICNICS AND PARTIES

Picnic Sausages

INGREDIENTS	Metric	Imperial	American
Large pork or beef			
sausages	*8*	*8*	*8*
Spring onions	*4*	*4*	*4*
Cream cheese	*50 g*	*2 oz*	*2 oz*
Mango chutney	*4 tsp*	*4 tsp*	*4 tsp*
Salt and pepper ground			
black pepper			

Grill the sausages, then allow to cool.

Roughly chop the spring onions and place in the blender. Add the cream cheese, cut into pieces, and the mango chutney. Blend, scrape down, season and blend again until well mixed.

Cut a wedge along the length of each sausage to remove a quarter of the sausage. Fill the gap made with the cream cheese mixture and then push the wedge of sausage back on top.

Wrap in foil to carry on a picnic.

NOTE
Do not freeze.

Breadcrumbs

Slightly stale bread can always be made into breadcrumbs and frozen until needed. Or they can be dried by laying the fresh crumbs out on a baking tray and placing this in the oven when some other food is being cooked. Once completely dry and cool, store in an airtight container until required.

INGREDIENTS
Bread

1. Cut the bread into cubes that will fit through the feed tube in the lid of the blender.
2. Drop the bread onto the revolving blades. Keep feeding bread in gradually until it stops being broken up. At this stage, stop and tip out the breadcrumbs, and start again with an empty blender.
3. Tip out and use as required. The crumbs can be coarsly chopped or made very fine according to how long they are blended for.

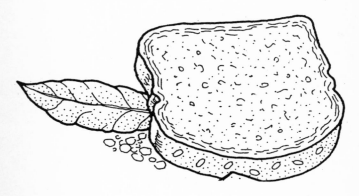

Crunchy Coated Chicken Drumsticks

 4 months

INGREDIENTS	Metric	Imperial	American
Chicken drumsticks	8	8	8
Bread	75 g	3 oz	3 slices
Peanuts	100 g	4 oz	¼ lb
OR *Cashews*	100 g	4 oz	¼ lb
Paprika	½ tsp	½ tsp	½ tsp
Freshly ground black pepper			
Coriander	1 tsp	1 tsp	1 tsp
Egg, beaten	1	1	1

Remove the skin from the chicken drumsticks.

Make the bread into crumbs in the blender. Remove. Chop the peanuts or cashews in the blender and add to the breadcrumbs. Add paprika and freshly ground black pepper and coriander. Mix well.

Dip the drumsticks in the beaten egg and then in the breadcrumb mixture. Bake at 190°C/375°F/Gas mark 5 for 20–30 minutes.

Vary the herbs and spices used: try adding 1 tsp of curry powder, or using 1 tsp dried rosemary or 1 tsp of dried thyme to replace the coriander.

TO FREEZE
Pack in a freezer container. Thaw for 4–5 hours at room temperature. Serve cold or reheat at 200°C/400°F/Gas mark 6 for 15 minutes.

Avocado and Tomato Dip

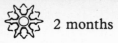 2 months

INGREDIENTS	Metric	Imperial	American
Small lemon	1	1	1
Ripe avocados	2	2	2
Garlic	1 clove	1 clove	1 clove
Cream	30 ml	2 tbsp	2 tbsp
Tomatoes	2	2	2
Tabasco sauce	few drops	few drops	few drops

Salt and freshly ground
  black pepper

Squeeze juice of the lemon and place in the blender.
Cut the avocados in half, remove the stones and
skin, and chop roughly. Place in the blender. Add
the clove of garlic, finely crushed, and the cream
and blend, scraping down if necessary.

Skin the tomatoes by making a small cut in the
skins and then pouring boiling water on top. Leave
for 1 minute, then pour off the water and add cold
water. Peel off the skin. Cut each in half and scoop
out the seeds. Reserve one half of one tomato for
garnish. Roughly chop the flesh of the rest and add
to the blender. Add the tabasco sauce and salt and
pepper and blend well. Taste and adjust seasoning.

Turn into a dish, garnish with strips of reserved
tomato, cover with cling film and chill for 30
minutes. Serve as a dip with vegetable sticks and
small savoury biscuits.

TO FREEZE
Pack into a freezer box. Thaw for 3–4 hours at
room temperature or overnight in the fridge.

NOTE

To prevent this discolouring, save the avocado stones and place on top of the purée when chilling. This will keep it looking the right colour for about 2 hours.

Bacon and Butter Bean Dip

INGREDIENTS	Metric	Imperial	American
Streaky bacon	*100 g*	*4 oz*	*¼ lb*
Tinned butter beans	*225 g*	*8 oz*	*½ lb*
Mayonnaise	*60 ml*	*4 tbsp*	*4 tbsp*
Lemon juice	*10 ml*	*2 tsp*	*2 tsp*

Derind the bacon, cut up finely and fry in its own fat until crisp.

Put the butter beans in the blender with the mayonnaise and blend. Add the bacon and lemon juice. Blend just long enough to combine.

Serve with celery sticks or other crisp vegetables to dip into it.

NOTE
Do not freeze.

Ham Cornets

INGREDIENTS	Metric	Imperial	American
Whole peppercorns	6	6	6
Bay leaf	1	1	1
Onion	1 small	1 small	1 small
Milk	200 ml	7 fl oz	1 cup
Flour	40 g	1½ oz	⅜ cup
Butter	40 g	1½ oz	3 tbsp
Salt and freshly ground black pepper			
Pâté	75 g	3 oz	3 oz
Butter	25 g	1 oz	2 tbsp
French mustard	½ tsp	½ tsp	½ tsp
Double (heavy) cream	60 ml	4 tbsp	4 tbsp
Ham	8 slices	8 slices	8 slices

Place the peppercorns, bay leaf and roughly chopped onion in the milk. Bring to the boil, remove from the heat and leave to infuse for 15–20 minutes. Strain the milk into the blender, add the flour and butter, blend and season well. Return to the pan and heat, stirring, until the sauce thickens. Pour it back into the blender and add the pâté, cut into pieces. Blend, then add the butter in pieces and the mustard. Allow to cool slightly then whip the cream and add to the blender. Blend just enough to fold in the cream.

Use the ham to line cornet moulds and support them upright by pushing them through holes in a cardboard cereal box. Place the mixture from the blender in a piping bag and pipe into each of the ham cornets. Chill for 1–2 hours. Alternatively, roll the ham into cones and secure with a cocktail stick, or spread the filling onto the ham slices and roll up. Arrange on a large plate and garnish.

NOTE Do not freeze.

Picnic Rolls

INGREDIENTS	Metric	Imperial	American
Wholemeal rolls	*6*	*6*	*6*
Chicken (cooked)	*175 g*	*6 oz*	*6 oz*
Bean sprouts	*175 g*	*6 oz*	*6 oz*
Butter, melted	*75 g*	*3 oz*	*6 tbsp*
Salt and freshly ground black pepper			

Choose large well rounded rolls — wholemeal or granary are best.

Cut off a lid from each roll and scoop out the middle, place in the blender and make into breadcrumbs. Remove. Chop the chicken, place in the blender and chop finely. Mix the chicken and bean sprouts. Add 6 tablespoons of the breadcrumbs to the mixture and pour in the melted butter. Season well. Fill the rolls with this mixture, packing in tightly. Replace the lids and cover completely with foil.

Warm in the oven at 200°C/400°F/Gas mark 6 for 20 minutes. Place in a box lined with kitchen roll and newspaper to keep them warm en route to the picnic.

Vary the filling according to taste: try chicken and pineapple, or minced beef and kidney beans, or minced lamb and coriander.

NOTE
Do not freeze.

Bacon and Pineapple Sandwiches

INGREDIENTS	Metric	Imperial	American
Streaky bacon	6–8 slices	6–8 slices	6–8 slices
Tinned pineapple	2 slices	2 slices	2 slices
Curd cheese	100 g	4 oz	¼ lb
Watercress	bunch	bunch	bunch
Brown bread	8 slices	8 slices	8 slices

Derind the bacon, grill until crisp and drain well.
Chop the pineapple slices roughly. Place in the
blender and purée. Add the curd cheese and blend
until well mixed. Spread the mixture on one side of
each slice of bread. Wash the watercress, dry and
place a generous layer on half the slices of bread.
Place the bacon slices on top of the watercress.
Turn the remaining slices of bread over, so the
cream cheese mixture is inside the sandwich and
place on top of the bacon. Press down well and cut
into triangles.

Makes 16 small sandwiches.

NOTE
Do not freeze.

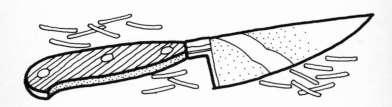

DRINKS

Lemonade

INGREDIENTS	Metric	Imperial	American
Lemon	*1*	*1*	*1*
Castor sugar	*25 g*	*1 oz*	*2 tbsp*
Water	*575 ml*	*1 pt*	*2½ cups*

Wash the lemon, cut it into quarters and place in the blender. Add the castor sugar and water and blend until well chopped. Strain into a jug and serve with plenty of ice and garnished with extra lemon slices.

Makes 3–4 glasses.

NOTE
Do not freeze.

Choose a thin-skinned lemon and allow the lemonade to strain without stirring or pressing the contents of the sieve, or the lemonade may taste bitter.

Pineapple Fruit Drink

INGREDIENTS	Metric	Imperial	American
Grapefruit	1	1	1
Orange	1	1	1
Lemon	1	1	1
Celery	1 stick	1 stick	1 stick
Tinned pineapple in natural juice	small tin	small tin	small tin
Water	120 ml	8 tbsp	8 tbsp
Crushed ice			

Squeeze the juice from the grapefruit and place in the blender. Cut the orange and lemon into 4, remove the flesh (without the white pith) and add to the blender. Cut the celery into pieces and place in the blender. Add the contents of the tin of pineapple and the water and blend until well combined and frothy. Pour into tall glasses with some crushed ice in each. Add extra fruits to garnish: use slices of lemon and orange or extra pineapple or grapes.

Makes 4 glasses.

NOTE
Do not freeze.

Banana Whip

INGREDIENTS	Metric	Imperial	American
Milk	425 ml	¾ pt	2 cups
Ripe banana	1 large	1 large	1 large
Ice cream	1 scoop	1 scoop	1 scoop

Place the milk in the blender. Add the chopped banana and the ice cream. Blend until frothy. Pour into tall glasses and add ice cubes.

Makes 2 glasses.

NOTE
Do not freeze.

Lemon and Lime Refresher

INGREDIENTS	Metric	Imperial	American
Lemon	*1 small*	*1 small*	*1 small*
Lime	*1*	*1*	*1*
Water	*575 ml*	*1 pt*	*2½ cups*
Sugar	*1 tbsp*	*1 tbsp*	*1 tbsp*
Mint	*few leaves*	*few leaves*	*few leaves*

Ice cubes

Wash the lemon and lime. Cut each into quarters and place in blender. Add the water and sugar and blend until foaming on top. Strain into a jug containing ice cubes and sprigs of mint. Serve immediately.

The amount of sugar may be increased according to taste. Choose thin-skinned fruit and allow to strain without stirring the pulp.

Makes 2 tall glasses.

NOTE
Do not freeze.

Hot Whipped Chocolate

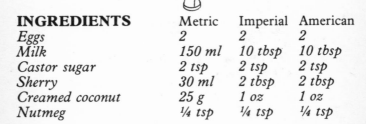

INGREDIENTS	Metric	Imperial	American
Water	*425 ml*	*¾ pt*	*2½ cups*
Good quality chocolate	*75 g*	*3 oz*	*3 oz*
Milk	*60 ml*	*4 tbsp*	*4 tbsp*
Whipping cream	*30 ml*	*2 tbsp*	*2 tbsp*
Cinnamon	*pinch*	*pinch*	*pinch*

Heat the water, and when hot but not boiling place it in the blender. Add the chocolate, broken up, and blend until smooth. Pour into a saucepan and bring to the boil. Simmer for 5 minutes. Return to the blender, add the milk and blend again until frothy. Pour into cups. Lightly whip the cream and float on top of the chocolate. Sprinkle with a little cinnamon. Sugar may be added to this recipe if required.

NOTE
Do not freeze.

Egg and Coconut Nog

INGREDIENTS	Metric	Imperial	American
Eggs	*2*	*2*	*2*
Milk	*150 ml*	*10 tbsp*	*10 tbsp*
Castor sugar	*2 tsp*	*2 tsp*	*2 tsp*
Sherry	*30 ml*	*2 tbsp*	*2 tbsp*
Creamed coconut	*25 g*	*1 oz*	*1 oz*
Nutmeg	*¼ tsp*	*¼ tsp*	*¼ tsp*

Wash one egg and place whole, including the shell, in the blender. Add the other egg without its shell, and the milk and sugar, and blend until frothy and smooth. Add the sherry and the coconut, cut into pieces, and blend again. Serve with a little freshly grated nutmeg on top.

Makes 2 glasses.

NOTE
Do not freeze.

Black Cherry Kir

INGREDIENTS	Metric	Imperial	American
Black cherries, tinned or			
bottled	*100 g*	*4 oz*	*¼ lb*
Water	*90 ml*	*6 tbsp*	*6 tbsp*
White wine	*275 ml*	*½ pt*	*1¼ cups*
Crushed ice	*2–3 tbsp*	*2–3 tbsp*	*2–3 tbsp*

Stone the cherries and place in the blender. Add the water and wine and 2–3 tbsp of crushed ice. Blend until well combined. Pour into tall glasses.

Makes 2 glasses.

NOTE
Do not freeze.

To crush ice cubes, place them in a plastic bag, cover with a tea towel and use a rolling pin to break up the ice cubes.

Iced Hawaiian Coffee

INGREDIENTS	Metric	Imperial	American
Tinned pineapple pieces	small tin	small tin	small tin
Milk	275 ml	½ pt	¼ cups
Instant coffee	5–10 ml	1–2 tsp	1–2 tsp
Hot water	10 ml	2 tsp	2 tsp
Vanilla ice cream	1 scoop	1 scoop	1 scoop
Sugar	1–2 tsp	1–2 tsp	1–2 tsp

Place the pineapple and juice in the blender and blend for 5–10 seconds. Add the milk and blend again. Mix the coffee with the hot water and add to the milk. Blend. Add the ice cream and blend until well mixed and slightly frothy.

Use pineapple pieces in natural juice if possible for this recipe. Add extra sugar only if needed; taste first, then sprinkle in sugar and blend for a few seconds.

Serve in tall glasses with ice cubes.

NOTE
Do not freeze.

BABY FOODS

These are quick and easy to make in the blender. At first foods can be completely puréed, and then as the baby can cope with coarser textures, so the food can be blended for shorter times.

Most home-made foods can be given to a baby, though it is wise not to add salt or sugar to baby foods. Also avoid egg whites for babies under eight months; use the yolk only. Very small babies are better with as little wheat products as possible, so avoid using flour or thickening. Formula milk, or expressed breast milk can be used to moisten foods that are too dry. Once over about six months, ordinary cows' milk can generally be used.

Many mothers find it worthwhile to cook complete meals for the baby, and then freeze the puréed food in ice cube trays. Once hard, the cubes of food can be placed in a plastic bag, and then defrosted as needed. Once the baby is a little older, ordinary family meals can simply be briefly blended as required.

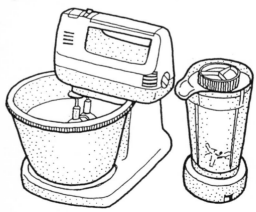

Chicken with Peas

 3 months

INGREDIENTS	Metric	Imperial	American
Chicken (cooked)	25 g	1 oz	1 oz
Frozen peas	25 g	1 oz	1 oz
Yoghurt or milk	10 ml	2 tsp	2 tsp

Chop the chicken roughly. Cook the peas in a little boiling water for 5 minutes Place the chicken, peas and yoghurt or milk in the blender and blend until smooth.

TO FREEZE
Pack into a freezer box. Thaw for 1–2 hours at room temperature. Heat in bowl over hot water.

Fish and Potato Lunch

INGREDIENTS	Metric	Imperial	American
White fish	50 g	2 oz	2 oz
Potatoes	1 med	1 med	1 med
Egg yolk	1	1	1

Poach the fish in a little water until soft. Cook the potato in boiling water until soft. Break up the fish, remove any skin and place in the blender. Add the cut up potato and the egg yolk and blend until smooth, scraping down as necessary.

NOTE
Do not freeze.

120

Cheese and Lentil Purée

 3 months

INGREDIENTS	Metric	Imperial	American
Lentils	75 g	3 oz	3 oz
Water	275 ml	½ pt	1¼ cups
Cheese	15 g	½ oz	½ oz

Soak the lentils according to the instructions on the packet, or use the no-soak variety. Place them in a pan with the water, bring to the boil and then simmer for 20 minutes until soft. Place in the blender, add the grated cheese and blend until smooth.

TO FREEZE
Cool, then pack into a freezer container. Thaw for 1–2 hours at room temperature. Reheat in a pan or in the oven at 200°C/400°F/Gas mark 6 for 10–15 minutes.

Banana and Yoghurt Dessert

INGREDIENTS	Metric	Imperial	American
Banana	1	1	1
Yoghurt	15 ml	1 tbsp	1 tbsp

Chop the banana roughly, place in the blender with the yoghurt and blend until smooth.

NOTE
Do not freeze.

Rice with Prunes

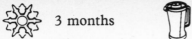 3 months

INGREDIENTS	Metric	Imperial	American
Pudding rice	*25 g*	*1 oz*	*1 oz*
Milk	*45 ml*	*3 tbsp*	*3 tbsp*
Prunes, tinned or dried			
and soaked	*25 g*	*1 oz*	*1 oz*

Cook the rice in the milk until soft, about 20 minutes. Remove the stones from the prunes, roughly chop and place in the blender. Add the cooked rice and blend until smooth.

TO FREEZE
Place in a freezer container. Thaw for 1–2 hours at room temperature. Serve cold, or reheat in a bowl over hot water.

Apple and Date Dessert

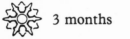 3 months

INGREDIENTS	Metric	Imperial	American
Dates	*50 g*	*2 oz*	*2 oz*
Lemon juice	*30 ml*	*2 tbsp*	*2 tbsp*
Eating apple	*1*	*1*	*1*
Water	*15 ml*	*1 tbsp*	*1 tbsp*

Chop the dates in the blender, place in a small pan with the lemon juice and heat until soft. Peel and slice the apple and stew in a little water until soft. Place both apple and dates in the blender, add 15 ml/1 tbsp of water and blend until smooth.

TO FREEZE
Place in a freezer container. Thaw for 1–2 hours at room temperature. Reheat in bowl over hot water.

INDEX